The Complete Photo Guide to

JEWELRY MAKING

Creative Publishing international

Copyright © 2010 Creative Publishing international, Inc.
First published in the United States of America by
Creative Publishing international, Inc., a member of
Quayside Publishing Group
400 First Avenue North
Suite 300
Minneapolis, MN 55401
1-800-328-3895
www.creativepub.com

ISBN-13: 978-1-58923-549-6
ISBN-10: 1-58923-549-5

10 9 8 7 6 5 4 3 2 1

Library of Congress Cataloging-in-Publication Data

Powley, Tammy.
  The complete photo guide to jewelry making : more than
500 large format color photos / Tammy Powley.
     p. cm.
  Summary: "Comprehensive guide to the tools and techniques
for making all types of jewelry"– Provided by publisher.
  ISBN-13: 978-1-58923-549-6 (soft cover)
  ISBN-10: 1-58923-549-5 (soft cover)
 1. Jewelry making. I. Title.

TT212.P6829 2011
739.27–dc22
                              2010027950

Copy Editor: Ellen Goldstein
Proofreader: Karen Ruth
Book Design: KimWinscher
Cover Design: KimWinscher
Page Layout: Danielle Smith
Photography: Corean Komarec,
    Michael V. Pawley, Rio Grande
Photography Coordinator: Joanne Wawra

Printed in China

Visit www.Craftside.Typepad.com for a behind-the-scenes
peek at our crafty world!

Due to differing conditions, materials, and skill levels, the
publisher and various manufacturers disclaim any liability for
unsatisfactory results or injury due to improper use of tools,
materials, or information in this publication.

The Complete Photo Guide to
JEWELRY MAKING

Creative Publishing
international

CONTENTS

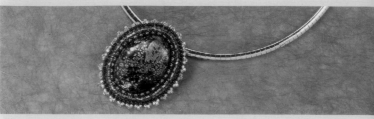

Introduction

Jewelry designing has become one of the most popular forms of crafting for both amateur artists and professional craftspeople. One reason for its popularity is that jewelry is a medium that can be enjoyed twice. Designers are first able to experience the pleasure of creating a jewelry piece and then have the opportunity to enjoy it again by wearing it rather than hanging it on a wall or setting it on a shelf, only to have to dust it at some point later.

No matter what your style, you will be able to find a type of jewelry that meets your needs. Plus, there are so many different methods for making jewelry it is just about impossible to master them all. This leads to broad possibilities in jewelry designing, and that is what this book is all about: visually showing, through a comprehensive guide of photographs, a variety of jewelry techniques available to all jewelry crafters. If you are a novice, you'll find an assortment of jewelry techniques to help get you started. For more experienced jewelry designers, the collection of jewelry methods presented may inspire you to try a new form of jewelry construction.

Along with techniques, plenty of projects are provided to illustrate how to combine these methods into finished jewelry pieces. However, don't limit yourself on this creative journey. Try the projects, and then experiment, play, and explore as you make your own jewelry designs using any number of techniques and materials included throughout the pages of this guide.

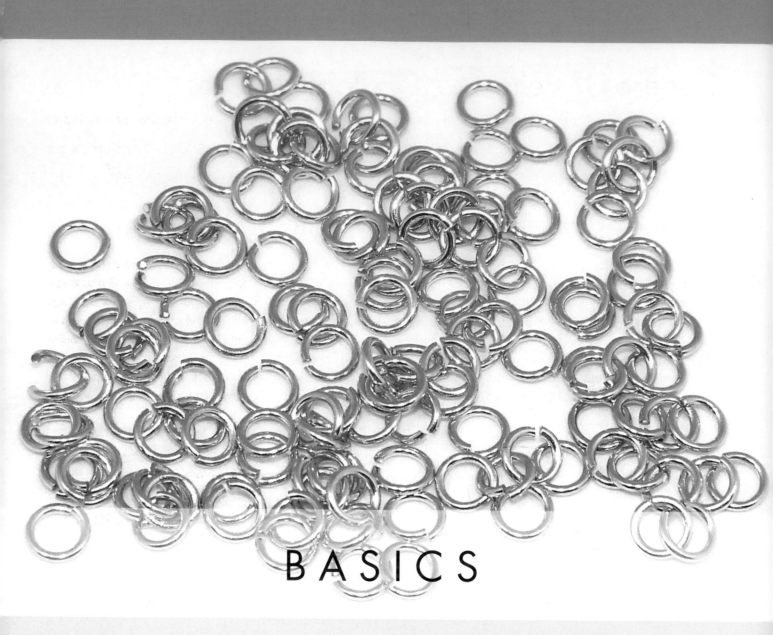

BASICS

Even though there are specialized tools and supplies required for specific types of jewelry making, a good number are also universal for the majority of jewelry techniques. If you are new to jewelry making, use this section to gain an understanding about the most common tools and supplies that are used for this very diverse craft. If you have tried a few jewelry-making techniques and want to discover more, refer to this section when you want to brush up on what you've already learned.

General Jewelry-Making Tools

This section discusses tools that just about all jewelry designers should have in their tool boxes and includes general uses for each one as well as tips for picking a quality tool. Most of these tools are available from jewelry supply vendors, bead stores, or craft stores (see Jewelry Supply Resources, page 298).

CHAIN-NOSE PLIERS

This particular tool is helpful for just about every type of jewelry making, from beading to fabricating. The nose is slightly rounded on the outside but flat and untextured on the inside. Chain-nose pliers are helpful for grasping materials as well as bending and shaping. Look for a pair with a spring handle, and make sure the handle is not too long to comfortably hold. The handles can range in length, usually around 5 to 6 inches (12.7 to 15.2 cm) long.

FLAT-NOSE PLIERS

These are very much like chain-nose pliers. Anyone working with wire, metal, and even beads will find these helpful—they provide an extra pair of fingers for bending material. They are most helpful when trying to make wider bends in metal than might normally be done with chain-nose pliers, but the distinction between the two pliers is marginal. The very subtle difference is in the shape of the pliers' nose, which is (as the name implies) flat.

BENT-NOSE PLIERS

These are very similar to chain-nose pliers when it comes to form and function. However, because they are angled about 45 degrees on the end, they feel more like an extension of your fingers when working with them.

ROUND-NOSE PLIERS

The nose on these pliers is rounded like two cones, which is helpful for curling wire as well as metal plate. As for all pliers, a spring handle is preferable, and the handles should not be too large to hold comfortably. The nose should be tapered as much as possible to allow for forming tiny curls using the end of the nose.

NEEDLE FILES

In general, needle files come in a set that includes different file shapes such as flat, round, half-round, square, and triangular. They are available in different lengths, but the small ones are about 5 inches (12.7 cm) long. Needle files resemble nail files, but the grit on these is much coarser and is designed for filing down the ends of wire or rubbing out scratches on sheet metal.

TUMBLERS

Tumblers are usually associated with polishing rocks, but they work well for cleaning metal. The traditional rock tumbler can be used for polishing either stone or metal. Magnetic tumblers are primarily used for cleaning metal, not tumbling stones. Both work basically the same using stainless steel shot, burnishing compound, water, and lots of tumbling to clean up metal. However, a rock tumbler can take hours while a magnetic tumbler can take minutes to do the same job. Another difference is in price. Rock tumblers are often much cheaper than magnetic tumblers.

WIRE CUTTERS

Wire-workers, fabricators, and even beaders will find a lot of uses for wire cutters. They are made to cut wire, but they are also useful for cutting beading wire, a form of stringing media. Try to get the flush-cut variety so that it leaves a flat end to any type of wire after cutting.

POLISHING CLOTH

A polishing cloth (not shown) is handy for all types of jewelry making. Even beaders can use it to shine up metal findings and beads.

POLISHING MACHINES

Hand-held rotary tools and polishing wheels are staples when it comes to cleaning and polishing all kinds of metals. When using a rotary tool (1), you will need a variety of abrasives, available separately or in a kit. The small mandrels that secure the abrasives insert into the rotary tool so that you can switch them in and out as needed while polishing. These work well for jewelry makers who may have just an occasional need to polish metal. For larger polishing jobs and more frequent needs, a polishing cabinet and motor (2) might be required. The cabinet has a fan that pulls small particles away from the jeweler while polishing, but it is always a good idea to wear safety equipment such as gloves, mask, and goggles.

SAFETY EQUIPMENT

Various types of safety equipment may be necessary to have on hand depending on the type of jewelry you plan to make. Always work in well-ventilated areas when dealing with torches or chemicals such as epoxy. Even simple polishing procedures can cause tiny particles to disperse into the air. Therefore, masks and respirators may be necessary to help protect your lungs. Eye protection may be necessary when working with certain types of equipment, such as polishers. Bits of metal and wire can fly off while cutting or forming. Heat resistant gloves are also a necessity when working with hot metals or kilns. Always read and follow safety instructions provided by manufacturers and vendors, and of course, use common sense when working with hazardous materials or equipment.

Jewelry Findings

Findings include items such as jump rings, bead tips, ear hooks, and clasps that allow you to connect components together to make a finished piece.

In the past, findings have been overlooked as the less glamorous side of jewelry making, but over the years, most designers' attitudes toward findings have changed because there is a larger assortment available, and unique findings can really add interesting details to finished jewelry pieces. In fact, it is even possible to make findings. This section includes an introduction to the various types of jewelry findings and their functions when it comes to connecting your jewelry designs.

EARRING FINDINGS

Fish or Shepherd Ear Hooks (1): These are some of the most common earring hooks. They are shaped in the form of a hook, and while the shape is the same, the design can vary. Some include a coil and ball above the loop of the hook, some have a flattened area around the curve of the hook, and some just have a loop on the end. All have loops on the end to attach a jewelry component.

Clip-ons (2): For those who don't have pierced ears, clip-on findings attach an earring to an earlobe. They also include loops to attach head pins or other dangle elements like charms.

Posts (3): Earring posts can come in a lot of different designs as well, but generally there is a stick through the

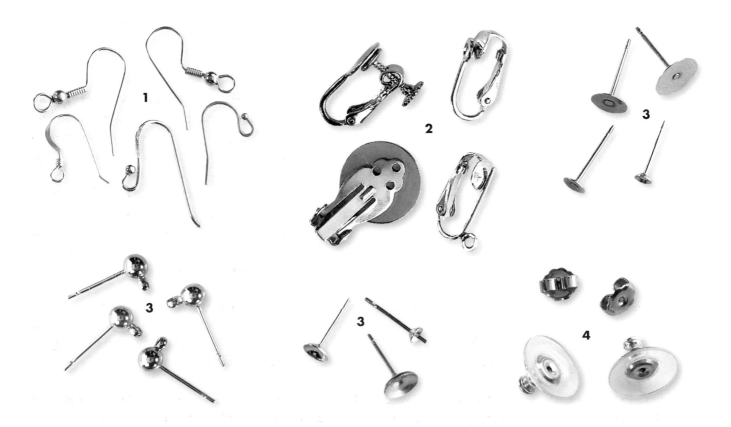

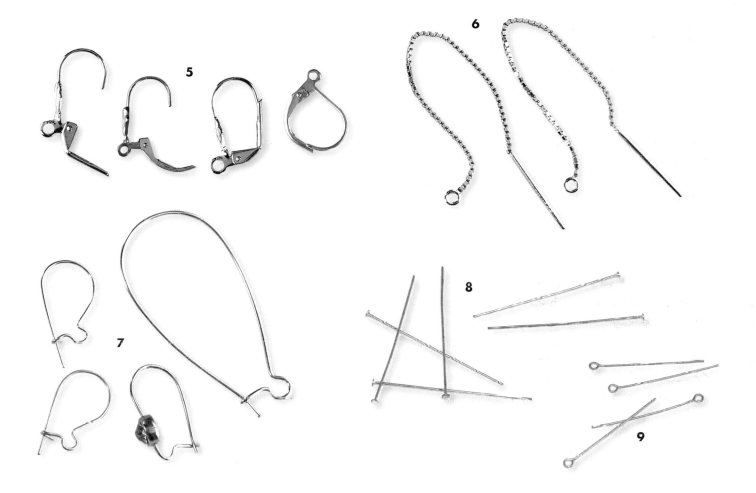

center of the piece that is used for attaching to an ear. Some posts are flat or curved on one end so that you can glue on beads or flat-backed items like cabochons. Others just include a metal ball over a loop so that you can attach a jewelry component to them.

Nut or Clutch (4): The back of an earring stick or post must be secured with a nut or clutch of some kind. These have a hole that the post fits through. They are available in metal as well as plastic.

Euro-Wires or Lever Backs (5): These are a little more upscale from the usual fish hook variety of earring findings. They have a hinge in the center that allows the hook to open and loops on the end for jewelry components.

Threaders (6): Called threaders or threads, these unique earring findings are made up of a loop (used to attach a

jewelry component) and a very thin chain and straight wire piece. To wear them, simply insert the straight piece and part of the chain through a pierced earlobe. They come in various lengths from 2 to 4 inches (5.1 to 10.2 cm) long.

Kidney Wires (7): These are also used to attach dangles in order to create earrings and are a similar shape to the fish hook style, but kidney wires have a small hook that allows you to attach the end of the ear hook and secure the earrings to the ears.

Head Pins (8): Used to add dangle elements to ear hooks, head pins are pieces of metal wire with one flat end that keeps beads from slipping off. The other end is used to loop and attach to the loop on an ear hook.

Eye Pin (9): These are just like head pins except one end has a loop or "eye" instead of being flat.

CLASPS

Spring Ring (1): These common clasps include a spring inside that allows them to open and close when the trigger is pressed. There is a loop on one side to connect to jewelry items.

Lobster Claw (2): These are very secure, and of course, look like the claw of a lobster. They have a loop on the end for attaching to jewelry and sometimes come with attached jump rings.

Hook and Eye (3): The hook-and-eye clasp comes in two parts: the hook and the eye. The hook attaches to the eye part of the clasp. These are primarily used with necklaces.

Toggle (4): This clasp also comes in two parts: the "T" shaped part and a circular part. To secure, simple insert the "T" into the circle.

Magnetic (5): These come in a lot of different designs, but all include two magnets that connect to create the closure for the clasp. They are useful for jewelry lovers who might have arthritis or other problems with their hands.

Slide Clasps (6): One side of this clasp connects by sliding into the other side. Most have multiple loops on each side to allow for multiple strands of beads.

Box Clasps (7): Very often, the box clasp is square, but it is available in other shapes, such as round and oval. One side has a hook that slides into the other side, which is the box part of the clasp.

Barrel Clasps (8): These also have two sides to them. The sides attach by one side screwing into the other side. They have loops on each end to connect to jewelry components.

CONNECTORS

Jump Rings: Used for wire, beading, and lots of other types of jewelry making, jump rings are round pieces of wire that form a ring. They can come unsoldered or soldered and are fairly easy to make (see pages 66 to 71). They have many functions such as helping to secure clasps or connecting to more jump rings to form chains.

Spring Rings: These look a lot like jump rings, but instead of the two ends meeting against each other, they pass each other so that they look like a small spring. They are often used to secure heavy charms or pendants.

Bails: The types of bails available vary greatly, but its primary function is to attach a component such as a charm or pendant onto necklaces, especially chains. Some bails are designed to attach to a component using a jump ring, while others may be attached with solder or embedded into a component.

BEAD STRINGING

Bead stringing is one of the most popular jewelry-making methods. The basics are easy to pick up, and considering the infinite types of beads available to jewelry designers, there are tons of designing possibilities. The process of arranging collections of beads in various patterns and color combinations makes this type of jewelry making very appealing. It is helpful to have a feel for color and form when creating bead strung jewelry.

Tools and Supplies

Along with some of the tools listed in the General Jewelry-Making Tools section such as chain-nose pliers, bead stringing requires a few specialty tools and supplies.

BEAD STRINGING TOOLS

Bead Board: Used for designing and determining the finished length of a strung piece of jewelry, a bead board is a board with one or more grooves to provide a place to arrange beads. Lines and numbers around the grooves indicate the length of the beads once strung together. This tool is very useful for moving beads around to determine the specific pattern before stringing as well as the final length.

Crimping Pliers: Crimp beads are best secured using a special tool called crimping pliers. These pliers have two notches in the nose that help fold and flatten the crimp bead around stringing medium such as beading wire. The inner notch is shaped like the letter U, and the outer notch is oval shaped.

Bead Reamer: Sometimes bead holes may be a little too small. A bead reamer is a pointed tool usually made from aluminum and textured with a diamond coating. By inserting the reamer into a bead hole and twisting, some of the bead's inner material can be removed, thus making the hole larger.

Beading Needles: There are a large variety of beading needles available for all kinds of beads and beading techniques. For typical bead stringing, a collapsible twisted needle is most often used. Once the threading medium is attached and the needle is inserted through some beads, the eye of the needle collapses, keeping it securely in place on the thread. These needles are stainless steel, disposable, and very inexpensive.

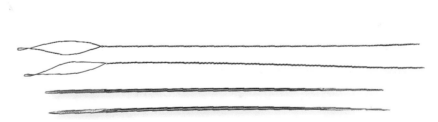

Awl: An awl is a pointed metal tool used primarily for creating knots between beads.

Bead Stopper: This handy gadget is used to keep beads from slipping off beading wire and other stringing media as you work. Simply pinch the ends to open up the spring in the middle, slip the string between a few of the coils, and release the ends.

Bead Tray: A shallow bowl works well for organizing beads and keeping them within reach while stringing.

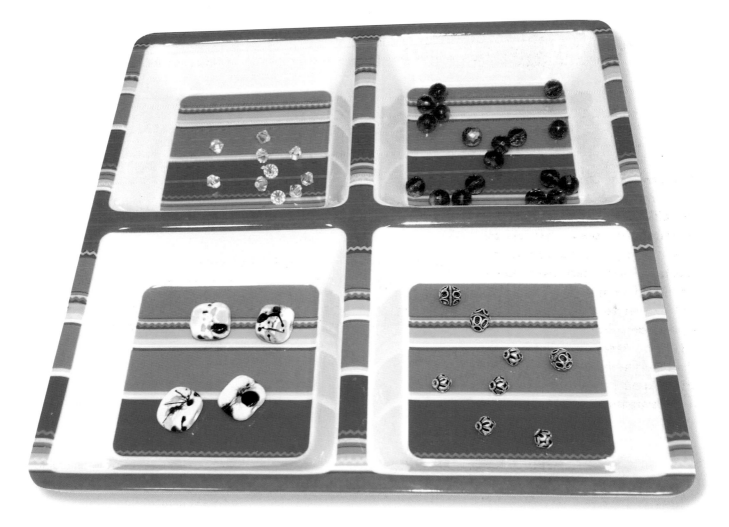

BEAD STRINGING SUPPLIES

Beading Wire: Unlike regular wire, beading wire is made of numerous strands of thin metal wire, such as stainless steel, that are then covered with a nylon coating. It is very flexible and strong and works especially well with heavy beads or beads, such as crystals, that might cut other types of threading medium. Beading wire is available in a number of diameters and colors.

Glue: When securing certain knots as well as attaching findings such as bead tips, glue is very handy. Hypo cement is one of the more popular beading glues.

Crimp Beads (1): Used to secure beading wire, crimp beads are either tube-shaped or round. The round crimp beads are normally only available in base metals. Tube-shaped crimp beads are easier to work with and more secure and come in metals such as silver, gold, gold-filled, copper, and brass. Though they can be flattened using chain-nose pliers, crimping pliers are designed specifically to secure crimp beads.

Crimp Covers (2): These are not necessary for assembling beaded jewelry, but they add a nice finishing touch. They cover the crimp bead, giving the appearance of a rounded bead rather than a folded crimp bead.

Bead Tips (3): These are also sometimes called clam shells because the double cupped variety has a similar appearance to a clam; they are used to secure knots on the end of strung jewelry such as necklaces. They also come with a single cup where the knot is exposed instead of hidden by the double-cup style.

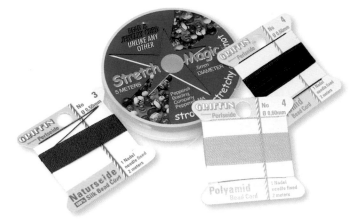

Nylon or Silk Thread: Traditionally, pearls are strung on silk thread; however, nylon is another good choice when stringing pearls or gemstone beads. Nylon and silk threads come in many colors and thicknesses. This is the type of thread used with collapsible needles, and it is even possible to purchase a few yards (meters) of thread with an attached needle.

Elastic Thread: Stretchy bracelets are very popular and are made with elastic thread. Elastic thread comes in many colors, including clear, and ranges in diameter from 0.05 to 1 mm.

BEADS

Of course, you need beads for bead stringing, and there is a wide variety available.

Gemstone: From amethyst to zebra stone, there is a gemstone bead available for every letter of the alphabet and then some. Very often, these come strung on monofilament that you then cut to access the beads.

Crystals: To add extra sparkle to any bead-strung piece of jewelry, crystals are the way to go. Swarovski is one of the better-known manufacturers of crystal beads, but there are lots of different types available. They come in all kinds of colors and also have various finishes such as aurora borealis (AB) or fire-polished, which creates a reflective rainbow effect.

Glass: Lampwork, pressed glass, furnace glass, Venetian glass, fused glass, seed beads, and African trade beads are all made from glass and are all very popular with bead stringers. Though the techniques for making glass beads vary, generally they are made by heating and forming pieces of glass, often in the form of glass rods. They may be created individually, which is done with lampwork beads, or they may be made from long tubes of glass and then cut, which is done with furnace and seed beads.

Pearls: Because of technological advances in pearl farming, pearl beads are very affordable, though the quality can vary depending on the grade of the pearl. AA pearls are very high quality and thus will cost more than B grade pearls. White is usually associated with pearls, but these days they come in all kinds of colors. Sometimes this means they have been dyed. They also come in lots of different shapes, not just traditional round pearls. Coin, teardrop, rice, semi-round, and stick are popular pearl shapes used in bead stringing.

Ceramic: Not just for pots, clay is a wonderful medium for beads as well. While many ceramic beads tend to use earth-tones, paints and glazes offer other color possibilities.

Natural Materials: Bone, horn, wood, and shells are a few examples of materials used to make beads. These types of beads are often strung with natural fibers, such as hemp and linen.

Polymer Clay: Make your own polymer clay beads or purchase them already made; either way this medium is known for unique color combinations. Polymer clay beads are another lightweight alternative to heavier beads such as gemstones.

Cloisonné: These beads are a combination of enamel and metal. They are created by firing enamel into intricate metal patterns on the beads. They look great by themselves but also work well combined with pearls and gemstone beads.

Plastic and Resin: For a lightweight pop of color, go for plastic or resin beads. Though plastic beads are more readily available in beads for children's projects, resin has come a long way, ranking among some of the most trendy bead choices. Because resin can be formed in all kinds of shapes and colors, the selection is plentiful.

Metal: Intricate detail is a characteristic of many metal beads. Balinese metal artisans are known for creating some amazingly detailed silver beads. Copper, gold, gold-filled, and even brass beads are also very popular. They work especially well as spacer beads between stone and crystal beads.

Techniques

There are only a few staple techniques beyond stringing and creating unique patterns and color combinations with the beads when it comes to assembling the jewelry pieces. The bead stringer needs to have the ability to finish off the ends of beaded items as well as secure portions of the beaded jewelry pieces. With some practice, these techniques are easily mastered.

CRIMPING WITH CRIMPING PLIERS

Crimp beads (page 21) are findings used to help finish off the ends of beaded jewelry pieces. While it is possible to simply use chain-nose pliers to flatten the crimp beads in place (and this is done by some bead stringers), to create a more finished look, use crimping pliers to secure crimp beads.

1 Insert one end of beading wire through a crimp bead and a clasp.

2 Take that same beading wire end and loop it back through the crimp bead, pushing the crimp bead down and pulling the bead wire so that there is still a loop of wire holding the clasp. Don't make this too tight. The clasp should be able to have some movement.

3 Double check that the beading wires are parallel to each other, and not crossed.

4 Grasp the crimp bead with the inner notch of the crimping pliers (the notch shaped like a U), and squeeze the handle, making sure to apply even pressure before releasing (A). This will fold or press the crimp bead into a U shape (B).

5 Turn the crimp bead so that the U is sideways (or C shaped), and grasp the crimp bead using the outer oval-shaped notch on the crimping pliers (A). Use even pressure and squeeze the handle to fold over the crimp bead (B).

6 Repeat the steps above to secure the second crimp bead to the other end of any jewelry piece.

YOU WILL NEED

- beading wire
- crimping pliers
- two crimp beads

4A

4B

2

5A

5B

Tip

To help ensure beading wire is evenly looped on both ends of a necklace or bracelet, insert the tip of a pair of round-nose pliers into the beading wire loop before securing the crimp bead. This also helps create even tension on the beading wire before closing up crimp beads.

SECURING CRIMP COVERS

Using crimping pliers to secure crimp beads adds a nice finishing touch that surpasses simply flattening them with chain-nose pliers. Consider covering crimp beads with crimp covers, small C-shaped findings that look like round beads when closed around a crimp bead. These do not necessarily provided any added security, but they look good and are easy to use.

YOU WILL NEED

- beading wire
- crimping pliers
- two crimp beads
- two crimp covers

1 Secure a crimp bead using the instructions opposite.

2 Place a crimp cover over the secured crimp bead.

3 Using the outside notch of the crimping pliers (the oval-shaped notch), grasp the crimp cover.

2

3

4

4 Gently squeeze the handle of the pliers in order to close the crimp cover. Check the crimp cover. When it is completely closed, it will look like a round bead with a seam down one side. If necessary, reposition the crimping pliers and close the bead up a little more. Do not use too much pressure, or you will end with a flattened crimp cover instead of a round one.

SECURING FIRST BEAD TIP

To finish off the ends of silk or nylon beading thread, bead tips (cup-shaped findings with attached hooks) work really well. For a beaded piece of jewelry, you will usually need two bead tips, one secured on each end. Though the techniques for securing bead tips on either end are similar, they vary slightly because the bead tips point in opposite directions. Therefore, securing them requires a few different steps. Securing the first bead tip is very easy to do.

2

3

YOU WILL NEED

- bead tip
- scissors
- beading thread (such as nylon or silk)
- collapsible beading needle
- glue
- chain-nose pliers

5

1 Attach a collapsible needle to the thread, or use thread that comes on a card with an attached needle.

2 Tie two overhand knots (page 206), one on top of the other, on the end of the thread, and use scissors to trim off excess thread.

3 Hold the bead tip so that the cup of the bead tip is facing toward the needle, and insert the needle and thread through the hole in the bead tip. Pull the thread until the knot rests in the cup of the bead tip.

4 Dab a small amount of glue onto the knot.

5 Use chain-nose pliers to close the bead tip cup around the knot.

Tip

Some beaders prefer to use clear nail polish as a substitute for glue.

SECURING SECOND BEAD TIP

After attaching the first bead tip and then stringing on the beads, the final step to securing the ends of a beaded piece of jewelry using bead tips is to add the second bead tip. Because this is on the opposite end of the jewelry piece, this technique requires a few altered steps compared to attaching the first bead tip.

YOU WILL NEED

- bead tip
- awl
- scissors
- beading thread (such as nylon or silk)
- collapsible beading needle
- glue
- chain-nose pliers

5

9

1 Once all of the beads are strung, insert the needle through the hole in the second bead tip, but make sure the cup is facing away from the needle.

2 Push the bead tip so that it rests up against the last bead strung.

3 Start forming a loose overhand knot, and insert an awl through the loose knot.

4 Continue to hold the awl through the knot, and with the other hand, pull the thread so that the knot tightens a little around the awl.

5 Still holding both the awl and the thread, use the awl to push the knot down into the bead tip cup.

6 Repeat steps 3 to 5 to form a second knot and push it into the bead tip cup.

7 Use scissors to trim off excess thread.

8 Dab a small amount of glue onto the knot.

9 Use chain-nose pliers to close the bead tip cup around the knot.

2

3

KNOTTING—2 STRANDS

Some call this the cheater's way to knot, but it works just fine for anyone who isn't ready to tackle the traditional knotting method just yet. It is also handy when holes in beads may be a little too large for the size of thread on hand. Knotting is best used with nylon or silk stringing medium, so it is good to finish the ends with bead tips.

YOU WILL NEED

- two bead tips
- scissors
- two strands of equally long beading thread (such as nylon or silk)
- two collapsible beading needles
- glue
- chain-nose pliers

1 Follow the same instructions for the Securing First Bead Tip technique, page 26, but instead of one needle and thread, use two and knot both ends of the thread together before securing the knot inside of the bead tip.

1

2

3

2 Once the bead tip is glued and closed, string on the first bead.

3 Push the bead up against the bead tip.

4 Now pull the thread strands apart, and start to tie a square knot (A) (right over left), using your fingers to push the knot up against the bead (B).

5 Finish the square knot, this time left over right (A), and again, push the knot up against the bead (B).

4A

5A

4B

5B

6

6 Repeat steps 3 and 4, adding a
bead and making a square knot
with both strands of thread, until the
jewelry piece is the desired length.

7 Finish the thread ends (again both
threads this time) using the Securing
Second Bead Tip technique,
page 27.

KNOTTING—1 STRAND

The purpose of adding tiny knots between beads is to keep them in place. This can be especially important if a necklace breaks so the beads won't go flying all over the place. Knots also keep porous beads (such as pearls) from bumping up against each other and possibly getting damaged. Knotting does take some time, but the final result is a secure, professionally finished necklace that has wonderful drape as well.

YOU WILL NEED

- two bead tips
- scissors
- awl
- one strand beading thread (such as nylon or silk)
- one collapsible beading needle
- glue

2

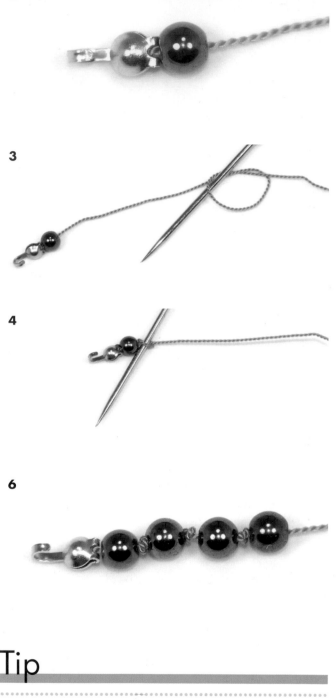

3

4

6

1 Follow the same instructions for the Securing First Bead Tip technique, page 26.

2 Once the bead tip is glued and closed, string on the first bead and push the bead against the bead tip.

3 Form a loose overhand knot, and insert an awl through it.

4 Continue to hold the awl through the knot and, with the other hand, pull the thread so that the knot tightens a little around the awl and then push the knot up against the previously strung bead.

5 While pulling the awl out of the knot, use your fingers to push the knot up against the bead.

6 Repeat steps 2 to 5, adding a bead and making a knot until the jewelry piece is the desired length.

7 Finish the end with another bead tip.

Tip

Dental floss or monofilament fishing line are not good substitutes for media made for bead stringing. Over time, they will stretch, often distorting the finished jewelry piece.

ELASTIC KNOT TECHNIQUE

Stretchy bracelets are always popular. When determining the size of a stretchy bracelet, it is a good idea to make it about an inch (2.5 cm) smaller than you would normally wear because the elastic stretches. So, if you wear a 7-inch (17.8 cm) bracelet, then you'll need enough beads to make a 6-inch (15.2 cm) bracelet.

YOU WILL NEED

- elastic jewelry thread
- beads
- scissors
- glue

1 Cut about 12" (30.5 cm) elastic jewelry thread, and string on your choice of beads.

Tip

When selecting beads for a stretchy bracelet design, make sure you have some beads that are at least 4 mm in size if you are using 0.05-mm elastic. It is also important to arrange the bead design so that the place where you form the knot is directly next to this or a larger bead. If the bead's holes are too small, the knot won't fit inside.

2 Tie a square knot with the elastic, right over left (A) and left over right (B).

3 Repeat, so that you have two knots, one on top of the other.

2A

2B

3

4 Use scissors to trim off excess elastic (making sure not to get too close to the knot), and dab a dot of glue onto the knot.

5 Before the glue has time to dry, pull on the elastic so that the knot gets pulled into the hole of one of the beads on either side of it.

6 Allow the glue to dry thoroughly according to the manufacturer's instructions.

4

5

Projects

The best way to practice bead stringing techniques is to go ahead and make some jewelry. Here are a few projects to get you started.

MINT JULEP LAMPWORK NECKLACE

Lampwork, metal, gemstone, and crystal beads make up this 20-inch (50.8 cm) beaded necklace design. The techniques used to make this project include Crimping with Crimping Pliers (page 24) and Securing Crimp Covers (page 25). The colors of the beads are reminiscent of a cool mint julep.

YOU WILL NEED

- 30" (76 cm) 0.014- or 0.015-mm clear beading wire
- eleven 15-mm Raku lampwork beads in shades of green and brown
- twenty-two 6-mm Swarovski peridot crystal beads
- twenty-four 4-mm natural mother-of-pearl beads
- twenty-four size 11 copper-colored seed beads
- twenty-two 5-mm sterling daisy spacer beads
- one 12-mm silver twisted toggle clasp
- two 2 × 2-mm silver crimp beads
- two crimp covers
- crimping pliers
- wire cutters

1

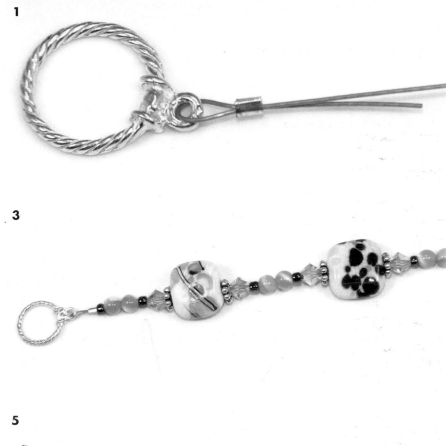

3

5

1. Attach one side of the toggle clasp to one end of the beading wire using a crimp bead.

2. Making sure to cover the beading wire tail with beads, start stringing beads in the following pattern: one copper-colored seed bead, two mother-of-pearl beads, one copper-colored seed bead, one peridot crystal bead, one silver daisy spacer bead, one lampwork bead, one silver daisy spacer bead, and one peridot crystal bead.

3. Repeat the bead pattern until all of the beads are used. The pattern should end with a copper-colored seed bead just like it began.

4. Attach another crimp bead and the other side of the toggle clasp to the end, making sure to insert a little of the beading wire tail through the last few beads.

5. Use wire cutters to trim off excess beading wire.

6. For a finishing touch add crimp covers to each end of the necklace.

6

FIRED UP ELASTIC BRACELET

Fire-polished crystal beads jazz up the wrist of anyone wearing this
sparkling crystal and pearl bracelet. Strung on elastic, it is easy to
toss on before heading out the door and comfortable to wear all day.
This project incorporates the Elastic Knot technique, page 31.

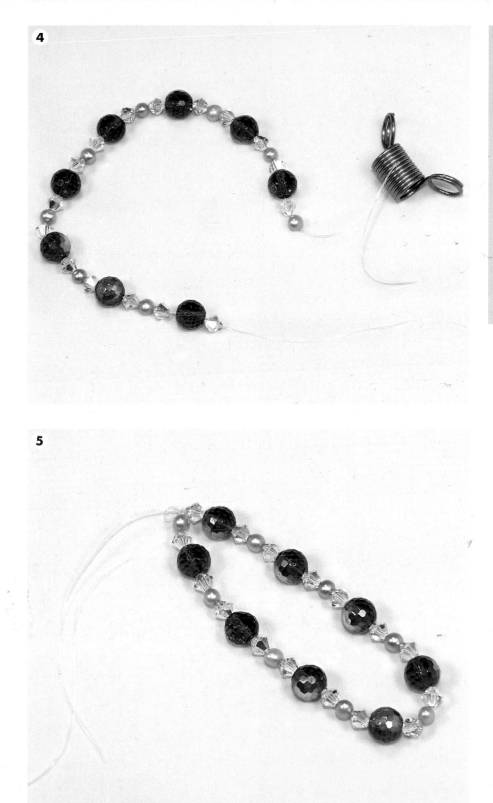

4

5

- eight 8-mm purple crystal fire-polished beads
- eight 3-mm purple pearl beads
- sixteen 4-mm Swarovski clear aurora borealis crystal beads
- one bead stopper
- 0.05-mm elastic jewelry thread
- scissors
- glue
- ruler

1 Measure out 12" (30 cm) of elastic thread and cut.

2 Attach a bead stopper to one end of the elastic.

3 String on beads in the following pattern: one pearl 3-mm bead, one clear 4-mm crystal bead, one purple 8-mm crystal bead, and one clear 4-mm crystal bead.

4 Continue to string on beads in this pattern making sure to end with one 4-mm crystal bead. The opposite end of the bracelet should start with one pearl bead.

5 Knot the elastic jewelry thread, trim off excess thread, dab the knot with glue, and pull the knot inside the 4-mm crystal bead.

6 Allow the glue to dry thoroughly before wearing the bracelet.

NOT YOUR CLASSIC KNOTTED BRACELET

Pearls are traditionally strung with knots between each pearl bead. Traditional knotting takes some practice, but with the Knotting—2 Strands technique, page 28, used for this pearl bracelet, very little practice is needed. As you tie each knot, make sure to keep the beading thread strands separate so they don't become tangled.

Knotting—2 Strands technique, page 28

YOU WILL NEED

- twenty 7-mm pale pink pearl beads
- two sterling silver bead tips
- scissors
- two number 2 light pink nylon beading threads with attached needles
- one 12 × 5-mm sterling silver filigree clasp
- glue
- awl
- chain-nose pliers

1 Take the ends of both beading threads and use two overhand knots, one on top of the other, to tie them together.

2 Secure a bead tip to the double strand knot, string a pearl bead onto both threads, and push the pearl bead until it is flush against the bead tip.

3 Pull the thread strands apart, and start to tie a square knot (A) (right over left), using your fingers to push the knot up against the bead (B).

4 Tie another knot with both strands, this time left over right, and push the knot up against the bead.

5 Add another pearl bead onto both threads, and push it up against the knot.

2

3A

3B

5

6 Repeat this process, adding a pearl bead and making a square knot with both strands of thread, until all the pearl beads except for one are strung and knotted.

7 Add the last pearl bead onto both strands, push it up against the last knot, and finish the end with another bead tip.

8 Finally, take one side of the filigree clasp, slip the loop part of the clasp onto the hook of one bead tip, and use chain-nose pliers to close the hook around the clasp.

9 Repeat the previous step to attach the other side of the clasp to the bracelet.

9

Tip

Good quality beads, findings, stringing materials, and tools will help you create jewelry that will last.

GEOMETRIC GEMSTONE AND PEARL KNOT NECKLACE

A good way to practice the Knotting—1 Strand technique, page 30, without taking on a major project is to scale back on the number of knots required for a jewelry piece. This design requires only two knots to help keep the beads in place, and the silk beading thread adds some corresponding color to the finished necklace.

YOU WILL NEED

- three 10-mm coin-shaped pearl beads

- two 10-mm square-shaped pearl beads

- twelve 4-mm light blue Czech fire-polished crystal beads

- six 6-mm lapis lazuli gemstone beads

- two sterling silver bead tips

- scissors

- one number 3 dark blue silk beading thread with attached needle

- one 10-mm square-shaped sterling silver toggle clasp

- glue

- awl

- chain-nose pliers

- ruler

1 Begin the necklace by attaching a bead tip to one end of the beading thread.

2

9

6

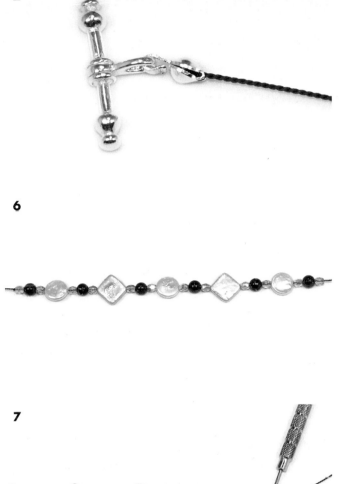

11

7

5 Repeat this bead pattern one time.

6 String on beads in the follow pattern: one crystal bead, one lapis bead, one crystal bead, one coin pearl, one crystal bead, one lapis bead, and one crystal bead.

7 Start forming a loose overhand knot, and insert an awl through it.

8 Continue to hold the awl through the knot and, with the other hand, pull the thread so that the knot tightens a little around the awl and then push the knot up against the previously strung bead.

2 Use chain-nose pliers to attach one side of the toggle clasp to the hook on the bead tip.

3 With a ruler, measure down 5" (12.7 cm) from the bead tip, and tie an overhand knot in the thread.

4 String on beads in the following pattern: one crystal bead, one lapis bead, one crystal bead, one coin pearl, one crystal bead, one lapis bead, one crystal bead, and one square pearl.

9 While pulling the awl out of the knot, use your fingers to push the knot up against the bead.

10 Measure 5" (12.7 cm) from the last knot just made, and attached a bead tip.

11 Use chain-nose pliers to attach the other side of the toggle clasp to the hook on the bead tip.

WIRE WORK

Wire is a versatile medium that is used in many types of jewelry making, such as fabrication and soldering. It can stand on its own or can be teamed up with other materials such as beads and found objects. Once the basics of wirework are mastered, there are all kinds of possibilities for constructing jewelry. Use wire for forming findings, connecting components, or creating wire-based jewelry designs.

Tools and Supplies

The majority of the tools needed for basic wirework are the same tools described in the General Jewelry-Making Tools, page 9: wire cutters, round-nose pliers, flat-nose pliers, chain-nose pliers, bent-nose pliers, files, and polishing equipment. However, there are a few additional tools that are very useful when working with wire. Jewelry wire is available in many sizes, shapes, hardness levels, and metal types.

WIRE-WORKING TOOLS

Rawhide Hammer: A rawhide hammer is also used to work harden or straighten wire. Because the head of the hammer is made from rawhide rather than metal, it will not mark the wire.

Nylon-Nose Pliers: The jaws on these pliers are made from nylon and are used to straighten and work harden wire. Grasp the wire with the nose of the pliers, and pull the wire through to straighten kinked wire.

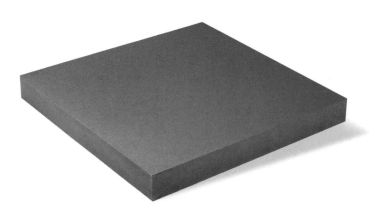

Bench Block: A steel bench block provides a solid surface when hammering wire.

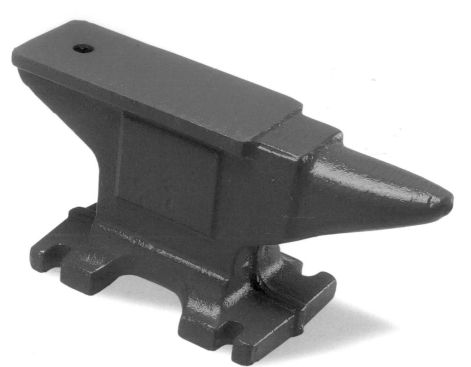

Anvil: An anvil works much like a bench block, but rather than being just a flat surface area to pound on, an anvil usually has at least one horn for shaping wire.

TYPES OF WIRE

Metals: Copper, brass, sterling silver, fine silver, gold-filled, and gold are just some of the metals wire comes in. For those with money to burn, it is possible to purchase platinum wire. Copper is great practice wire because it is so inexpensive. Red brass wire is also a good alternative to gold; it has the look without the cost. Finally, sterling silver is a staple wire found in most wire-workers' tool boxes. Fine wire has its purposes, but since it is almost pure silver and has very little alloy, it is a lot softer than sterling silver and doesn't always work well for some wire applications.

Shapes: Round wire is the most universal when it comes to wire techniques; however, square, triangle, and half-round wire are also available and have some practical uses both in wire work and metal fabrication. For example, half-round wire works well when wrapping wire sections together, especially square wire. It is a good idea to experiment with different shapes of wire rather than to assume one shape is designed for one purpose.

Colors: Wire comes in green, red, blue, and purple—just about every color of the rainbow. Colored wire is made a few different ways, depending on the manufacturer, but usually it has a base-metal core with a color coating on the outside of it. Some coated wires can be easily marked with metal tools, so nylon tools are recommended for best results.

Size: The size of the wire is called the gauge, and it is determined by its diameter. The thinner the wire, the larger gauge number it will have. For example, 21-gauge (0.724 mm) is thinner than 16-gauge (1.29 mm) wire. For most basic wire work, the wire sizes to have on hand are 24-, 21-, and 20-gauge (0.5, 0.72, and 0.80 mm).

These sizes work with a range of jewelry components, such as beads, and are also useful for making basic findings, such as earring hooks and clasps.

Hardness: Wire comes in dead-soft, half-hard, and full-hard. The hardness is determined by the number of times it has been pulled through a drawplate. The more it has been pulled, the harder it becomes. Dead-soft is the softest and full-hard is the hardest. Hard wire may be strong but very difficult to work with considering the fact that the wire-worker often has just a few hand-tools to manipulate the wire. It is rare that full-hard wire is used in wirework. Half-hard is a good in-between wire and works well for items that may have to sustain some weight, such as a clasp. Dead-soft is the easiest of the three to bend and shape, and as it is manipulated, it will become work hardened (see page 44) a little; however, it may be too soft for heavy jewelry pieces. When picking the type of wire you want to use, think about how heavy the finished piece will be. Lightweight jewelry pieces are often fine with dead-soft wire. Heavy jewelry pieces may need a little more hardness, and half-hard would be the best choice.

Techniques

The purpose of most wire techniques is to create what is called a "cold connection," meaning connecting items together without the use of heat (such as from a soldering iron). By manipulating the wire, you can connect other wire components as well as beads, pendants, or charms. Wire is also very handy for making components such as findings, which is ideal for those jewelry designers who want to add an extra layer to their handcrafted jewelry designs.

WORK HARDENING WIRE

The more wire is manipulated, the harder it will become. There are a number of simple ways to harden wire, including using a rawhide hammer and anvil or bench block or pulling wire through the jaws of a pair of nylon-nose pliers.

YOU WILL NEED

- wire of your choice
- nylon-nose pliers
- rawhide hammer
- anvil or bench block

1 For work hardening with nylon-nose pliers, hold the end of the wire with your fingers, grasp the wire just above this area with the jaws of the pliers, and as you continue to hold onto the wire with your fingers, pull the pliers down the length of the wire.

1

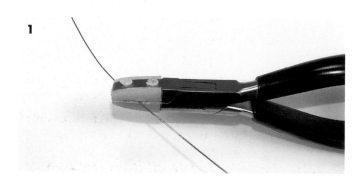

3

4

2 Repeat this a few times. The more the wire is pulled, the harder it will become.

3 For work hardening with a hammer, place the wire or wire component you want to harden on the top of an anvil or bench block.

4 With a rawhide hammer, hit the wire piece a few times. It doesn't take a huge amount of force; a good firm tap usually works.

5 Repeat this a few times. The more the wire is hit, the harder it will become.

FILING WIRE

The ends of wire pieces can become sharp after being cut with wire cutters, so needle files are useful for flattening the ends and removing any burs or sharp areas that can scratch the wearer. If a jeweler uses a sharp pair of flush-cut wire cutters, this cuts down on the amount of filing required. When determining which areas of wire to file or not file, think about what sort of contact the jewelry wearer will have with the wire component in question.

YOU WILL NEED

- wire of your choice
- needle file

1 Grasp the piece of wire in one hand and a file in the other hand.

2 While holding the wire straight up, file the end in one direction, not back and forth.

3 Repeat filing in one direction until the wire end is flat and smooth to the touch.

2

Tip

After completing a piece of wire jewelry, take a few minutes to feel around the different areas where the wire has been cut. If any of them are sharp, file them a little more.

WIRE COIL

Wire coils can be used functionally or decoratively. Form a coil at the end of a piece of wire to create a jazzed-up head pin or finish the ends of the wire with a coil to create an ornamental effect.

YOU WILL NEED

- choice of wire
- round-nose pliers
- nylon-nose pliers

1 Use round-nose pliers to make a small curl on the end of the wire.

2 Grasp the curl with nylon-nose pliers, hold the straight part of the wire with your fingers, and continue to curl the wire to form a coil.

3 Continue to coil the wire until you have the size you desire.

1

2

Tip

Use the coiling technique to make your own head pins ahead of time and stash them away for later use.

END OF WIRE UNWRAPPED LOOPS

Without the aid of soldering, a simple loop in a wire can connect all types of jewelry components from dangles to charms. These instructions explain how to make a small unwrapped loop that is about ⅛ inch (3 mm) in diameter, but the loop can be a variety of sizes depending on what it will be used to connect.

YOU WILL NEED

- wire of your choice
- round-nose pliers
- chain-nose pliers
- ruler

1 About ⅜" (9 mm) from the end, bend the wire at a 90-degree angle with a chain-nose pliers.

2 Grasp the bent area with round-nose pliers, and curl the wire toward you to form a loop.

1

2

LONGER WIRE UNWRAPPED LOOPS

This is basically the same technique as the End of Wire Unwrapped Loops method, but sometimes it is necessary to put an unwrapped loop on a long piece of wire or very often at the top of a head pin that may be a few inches (centimeters) long. While it is possible to cut off the longer piece of wire or head pin and make the unwrapped loop on the end of it, this is an alternative that ensures nice round loops. You will learn how to make an unwrapped loop on a head pin that holds a bead.

YOU WILL NEED

- head pin
- bead
- round-nose pliers
- chain-nose pliers
- wire cutters

1 Just past the bead on the head pin, use chain-nose pliers to bend the wire at a 90-degree angle.

2 Grasp the bent area of wire with round-nose pliers, and using your fingers or chain-nose pliers, wrap the wire around the nose of the pliers.

3 Use wire cutters to trim off the head pin right at the point that the loop ends.

2   **3**

WRAPPED LOOPS

When a little extra security is needed for a cold connection, a wire-wrapped loop is the way to go. It is very similar to the unwrapped loop technique, only the loop is secured by wrapping the wire around itself. Wrapped loops can also be formed in various sizes depending on their function in a jewelry design.

YOU WILL NEED

- wire of your choice
- round-nose pliers
- chain-nose pliers
- ruler
- wire cutters

1 About 1" (2.5cm) from the end, bend the wire at a 90-degree angle with chain-nose pliers.

2 Grasp the bent area of wire with round-nose pliers, and using your fingers, wrap the wire around the nose of the pliers.

3 Keep the pliers' nose inside the loop created in the previous step, the shorter piece of wire pointing straight up, and your pointer finger pressing against the loop of wire on the nose of the pliers.

1

2

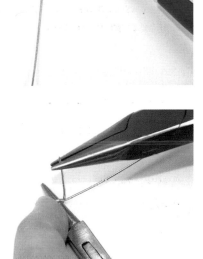

4

5

4 Grasp the short piece of wire with chain-nose pliers, and start wrapping the short piece of wire around the longer piece of wire.

5 Continue to wrap as many times as you'd like. If you only want a few wraps, trim off excess wire with wire cutter.

WIRE HOOK

Next to cold connection, making findings is another excellent use of wire. A wire hook is one of the most versatile and easy findings to make. For heavy jewelry pieces, wire as thick as 16- or 18-gauge (1 mm) is recommended. For lighter jewelry designs, 21-gauge (0.7 mm) dead-soft is fine as long as it is work hardened a little. Half-hard wire in various gauges is also a good choice since it will not require work hardening like softer wire. Choosing wire thickness is based on common sense. Heavy jewelry pieces will require heavier hooks than lighter jewelry pieces will.

YOU WILL NEED

- 2" (5 cm) of 21-gauge (0.7 mm) wire
- round-nose pliers
- nylon-nose pliers
- chain-nose pliers
- ruler
- bench block or anvil
- rawhide hammer

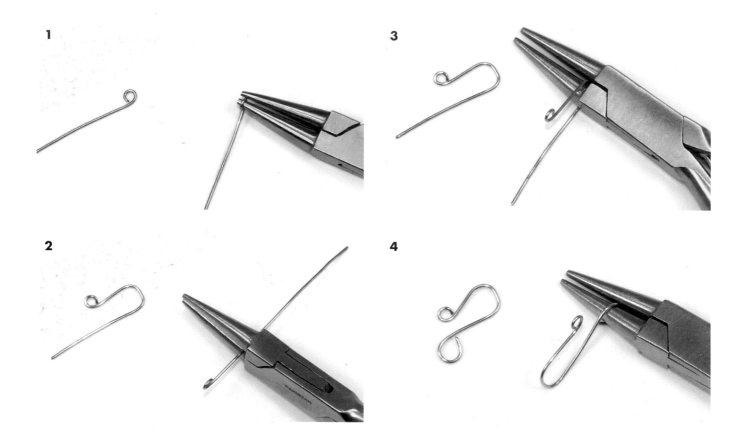

1 Use round-nose pliers to form a small curl on one end of the wire.

2 About ½" (1.3 cm) down from the curl, use the thickest area of the round-nose pliers to grasp the wire piece.

3 Use your fingers to push the wire down and around the nose of the pliers. Squeeze the wire around the nose to help the bent wire form a round shape.

4 Using the middle area of the pliers' nose, make another larger curl on the opposite end of the wire piece.

5 If the wire is dead-soft, work harden it a little.

5

Tip

To keep wire from oxidizing too quickly, store it in a zippered plastic bag and label it with the gauge number and type of metal. If it gets a little dark, just wipe it a few times with a polishing cloth.

FIGURE 8 "EYE" COMPONENT

1

Primarily this simple component, shaped like the number 8, is used as a connection for a hook or other types of clasps. Though, of course, with some imagination lots of other uses can be found for this wire finding, such as joining a number of them to form a chain or create dangles.

YOU WILL NEED

2

- 1½" (3.8 cm) of 21-gauge (0.7 mm) wire
- round-nose pliers
- nylon-nose pliers
- chain-nose pliers
- bench block or anvil
- rawhide hammer

3

1 Using the thicker area of the round-nose pliers, make a larger curl on one end of the wire piece.

2 Flip the wire piece, and repeat the previous step but orient the curl in the opposite direction

3 If the wire is dead-soft, work harden it a little.

WIRE-WRAPPED BEAD

Combine wrapped-loop techniques with a bead to create an interesting effect. Use this on all shapes of beads and types of metal. It takes a little more time than just adding the wire loops on each end of a bead, but the results are worth it. The amount of wire needed will depend on the size of the bead, but it is better to have a little too much than not enough. You can always trim off any excess.

YOU WILL NEED

- wire and bead of your choice
- round-nose pliers
- nylon-nose pliers
- chain-nose pliers
- wire cutter

1 First make a wire-wrapped loop (page 47) on the wire, and then slip on your choice of bead.

2 On the opposite end of the bead, start another wrapped loop (A) and wrap the wire around itself a few times (B). Do not trim off excess wire.

3 Take the extra wire, and bring it down across the bead.

4 Wrap the wire around the wire-wrapped loop created in step 1.

5 Continue to wrap the wire around a few times, and if necessary, trim off excess wire.

2A

2B

3

4

5

6 Use chain-nose pliers to press and flatten the wire against the wire wraps.

WIRE-WRAPPED BRIOLETTE

Teardrop-shaped beads that have the hole drilled through the side rather than from top to bottom are called briolettes. Wrap them with a little wire to create dangle elements for elegant earrings or add them to a necklace for an unexpected design element. Make sure the wire you select fits through the hole in the briolette. Sometimes these types of beads can have fairly small holes, so thin wire (usually around 24-gauge or 0.5 mm) may be necessary.

YOU WILL NEED

- wire and briolette bead of your choice
- round-nose pliers
- chain-nose pliers
- bent-nose pliers
- wire cutters

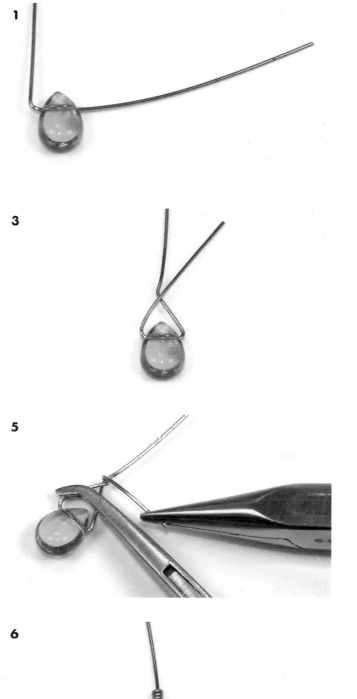

1 About 1½" (3.8 cm) down the wire, bend the wire at a 90-degree angle with the chain-nose pliers, and slip on the briolette bead.

2 Use chain-nose pliers to bend the other end of the wire at a 45-degree angle over the bead, and then right above the bead, bend it again so the wire is pointing straight up.

3 Bend the 1½" (3.8 cm) side of the wire a little more so that it is also at a 45-degree angle and crossing over the other end of the wire just under where the wire bends to go straight up.

4 Use bent-nose pliers (an extra pair of chain-nose pliers will work too) to grasp both wire sections just past the point of the briolette.

5 As you hold the wires with bent-nose pliers, use chain-nose pliers to wrap one wire over the other.

6 Continue to wrap the wire a few times, and use wire cutters to trim off excess wire.

Projects

After loading up on techniques, it is time to consider making a few pieces of wire jewelry. These projects were designed to use a combination of the techniques previously described. Some of them, like those using wrapped loops, can take a little practice, so consider using inexpensive practice wire such as copper or brass before breaking out the good stuff.

CARNELIAN COIL PENDANT

One oval carnelian bead and a little red brass wire combined with coiling and wrapped loops is all you need to make this gemstone pendant. Attach it to a chain, or make two and add ear hooks for a pair of wonderful earrings. This project shows how the Wire Coil technique can be both pretty and practical at the same time.

YOU WILL NEED

- 6" (15 cm) of 21-gauge (0.724 mm) dead-soft brass wire
- one 15 × 20-mm oval-shaped carnelian bead
- round-nose pliers
- nylon-nose pliers
- chain-nose pliers
- ruler
- wire cutter

1 Make a coil (page 45) on the end of the wire, and use chain-nose pliers to bend the wire just past the coil so that it is standing straight up.

2 Slip the carnelian bead onto the wire, and push it down so it is up against the coil.

3 Form a wrapped loop (page 47) at the top of the bead (A). You will have a good deal of extra wire. That is fine. Do not trim it off (B).

4 With the leftover wire, form a coil and continue to coil it up until it is about a ½" (1.3 cm) away from the wrapped loop.

5 Use your fingers to push the coil flat up against the front of the bead.

3A

3B

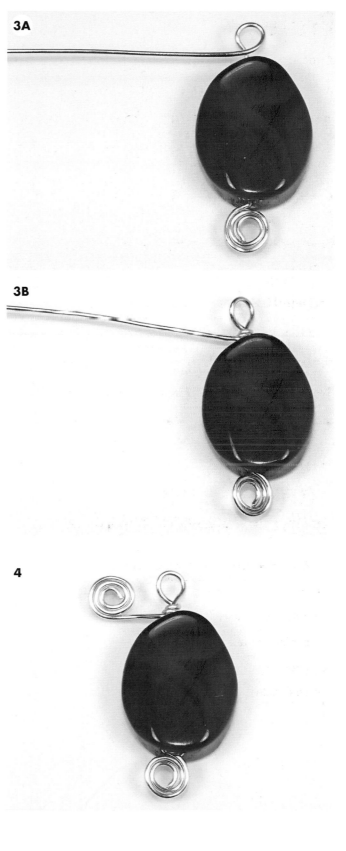

1

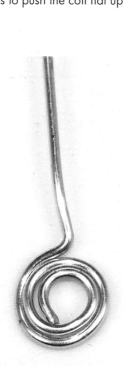

4

Tip

Save scraps of wire, especially sterling and gold-filled. Many vendors who sell wire will buy back scraps and/or give customers credit.

WRAP IT UP NECKLACE

Lots of wirework is going on in this dynamic and chunky necklace. Round beads are not the only types of beads that can be wrapped with wire. Square turquoise beads wrapped with sterling wire provide a contrast next to the sterling and crystal sections in between each wrapped bead. This piece combines the Wrapped Loop, Wrapped Bead, and Hook-and-Eye techniques.

YOU WILL NEED

- 60" (1.5 m) of 21-gauge (0.724 mm) sterling round dead-soft wire
- 2" (5 cm) of 20-gauge (0.8 mm) sterling round half-hard wire
- 1½" (3.8 m) of 20-gauge (0.8 mm) sterling round half-hard wire
- ten 4-mm Swarovski crystal round clear aurora borealis beads
- five 12-mm sterling Bali-style beads
- six 25-mm reconstituted turquoise square beads
- twelve 5 mm sterling jump rings
- round-nose pliers
- nylon-nose pliers
- chain-nose pliers
- ruler
- wire cutter
- needle-nose file

1

2

1 Begin by taking 6" to 8" (15 to 20 cm) of 21-gauge (0.7 mm) wire, make a wrapped loop (page 47) on one end of the wire, and thread on a turquoise bead.

2 Make another wrapped loop on the other end of the wire, and bring the extra wire up and over the bead in order to start the wrapped bead technique (page 50).

3 Wrap the wire around the previous wrapped loop once, and then bring the wire back down over on the other side of the bead.

(continued)

4 Wrap the wire around the previous wrapped loop a few times so that the wire is now wrapped around both sides of the bead.

5 Trim excess wire, use chain-nose pliers to press the wire end flat, and if necessary, file the wire end smooth.

6 Repeat steps 1 to 5 for all the other turquoise beads.

7 With about 4" (10 cm) of 21-gauge (0.7 mm) wire, make a wrapped loop on one end, and thread on one crystal bead, one sterling bead, and another crystal bead.

8 Make another wrapped loop on the other end of the wire.

9 Repeat steps 7 and 8 for all the other sterling and crystal beads.

4

7

5

8

10

11

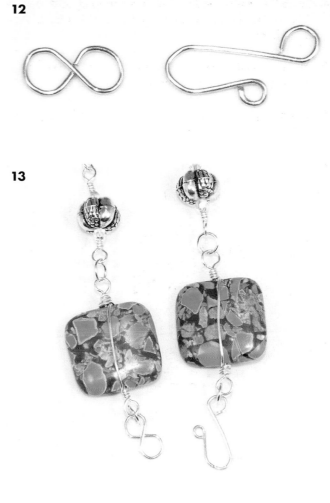

10 Now start to connect the bead sections using jump rings. Use chain-nose pliers, open one jump ring, and slip the loops of one turquoise bead section and one sterling bead section onto the jump ring. (See pages 66 to 72 for instructions on making jump rings as well as opening and closing them properly.)

11 Continue connecting all the other turquoise and sterling bead sections together with jump rings.

12

13

12 Use 20-gauge (0.8 mm) sterling wire to make a hook and eye (page 48).

13 Connect the hook and eye to either end of the connected bead sections using jump rings.

Tip

It is always easier to work with longer pieces of wire, anywhere from 6 to 12 inches (15 to 30 cm), than short pieces of wire. So if instructions indicate only a few inches (centimeters) are needed, cut a larger piece and just trim off any excess. Leftover wire can be recycled or used for future projects.

SMOKY BRIOLETTE AND PEARL EARRINGS

Nothing denotes elegance like pearls and briolette beads. The smoky-colored facets of the briolettes set off the pale peach pearls. These earrings use the Unwrapped Loop and Wire-Wrapped Briolette techniques.

YOU WILL NEED

- 12" (30 cm) of 24-gauge (0.5 mm) sterling round dead-soft wire
- two 10 × 20-mm smoky-colored faceted briolette beads
- two 5-mm light peach pearl beads
- four 4-mm sterling daisy spacer beads
- two sterling ear hooks
- round-nose pliers
- nylon-nose pliers
- chain-nose pliers
- wire cutters

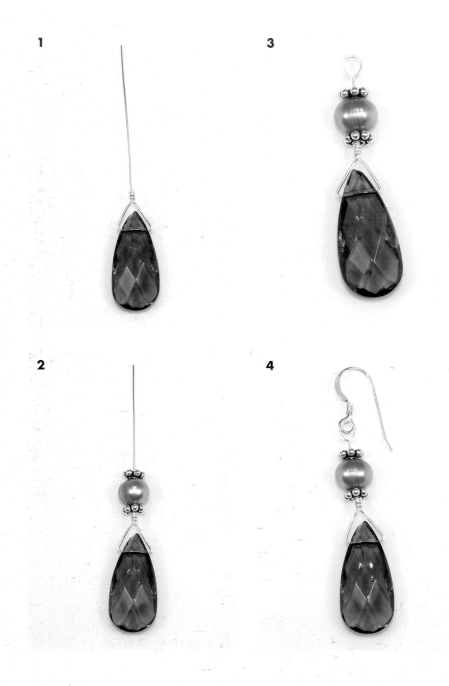

1

2

3

4

1 Start with about 6" (15 cm) of sterling wire, and use the wire-wrapped briolette technique (page 51) to attach the wire to one briolette bead.

2 Thread one daisy spacer bead, one pearl bead, and another daisy spacer bead onto the wire. (You may want to straighten the top part of the wire a little with nylon pliers if it is bent.)

3 With round-nose pliers, make an unwrapped loop (page 46) at the top of the wire, trimming off any excess wire with wire cutters.

4 Add an ear hook to the unwrapped loop, and use chain-nose pliers to ensure the unwrapped loop is closed securely around the ear hook.

5 Repeat steps 1 to 4 in order to make another earring so that you have a matching pair.

SPARKLING EARTH EARRINGS

Earth-toned copper wire and bamboo beads are an unusual combination with Swarovski glitter and glam crystals in these earrings that you can wear to the office or to the local Earth Day celebration. The techniques used in this project include Unwrapped Loops and the Wire Coil technique.

YOU WILL NEED

- 12" (30 cm) of 21-gauge (0.7 mm) copper round dead-soft wire
- two 8-mm topaz-colored aurora borealis Swarovski crystal beads
- two 12 × 7-mm bamboo beads
- four 4-mm goldstone beads
- two gold-filled ear hooks
- round-nose pliers
- nylon-nose pliers
- chain-nose pliers
- wire cutters

1 With about 6" (15 cm) of wire, make a coil (page 45) on the end of the wire, and slip on one crystal bead.

2 Make an unwrapped loop (page 46) at the top of the crystal, trimming off excess wire as necessary.

3 Using the rest of the wire, make an unwrapped loop on the end, and thread on one goldstone bead, one bamboo bead, and one goldstone bead.

4 Add another unwrapped loop on the other end of the wire, trimming off excess wire as necessary.

5 Connect the crystal bead section to the bottom of the bamboo bead section.

6 Add an ear hook to the top of the bamboo bead section.

7 Repeat steps 1 to 6 in order to make another earring for a matching pair.

1

3

2

4

6

CHAIN MAKING

The heyday of chain making dates back to the days of chain maille when small links of metal were connected together to form chains as well as protective body armor. The technology behind chain making is relatively basic: wire is formed into links and then connected together. In jewelry making, the links are also called jump rings. Once enough jump rings are made, the only other skill required is to connect them together. For most chain making, no soldering is required as long as the jump rings are made well and attention is paid to the ratio of wire diameter to mandrel diameter; this will ensure strong jump rings that do not come apart. The more precisely jump rings are cut, the better quality the rings and the more secure the finished chain will be once all of the rings are connected.

Tools and Supplies

Many of the tools discussed in the General Jewelry-Making Tools section are needed for making chains including chain-nose pliers or flat-nose pliers, wire cutters, needle files, and polishing machines or tumblers. Other tools required have more than one function in jewelry making and are more than worthy of space on any jeweler's workbench.

Heavy-Duty Wire Cutters: Though wire cutters are already included in the General Jewelry-Making Tools section, it is a good idea to have a few different pairs depending on the gauge of wire used. For heavy gauge wire, heavy duty wire cutters are needed; otherwise, the thick wire can quickly dull and even damage lighter weight wire cutters.

Dowels or Mandrels: Dowels or mandrels are necessary to form uniform jump rings. The diameter of the mandrel will determine the finished size of the jump ring, so it is a good idea to have a range of sizes. To get started, a pencil or a knitting needle will do the trick. Wooden dowels can be purchased at most hardware stores, and metal mandrels are available from jewelry tool vendors.

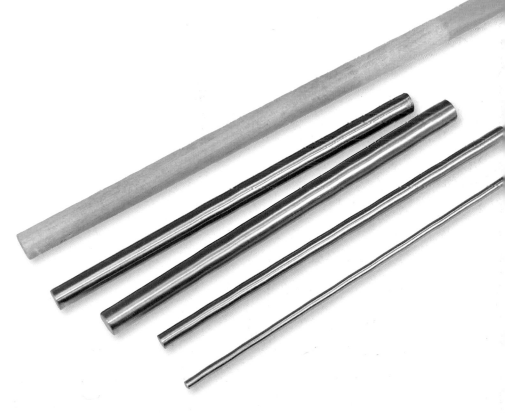

Jeweler's Saw: A jeweler's hand saw is used to cut wire rings and metal sheet. The frame of the saw is designed to fit interchangeable saw blades on one side. Most metal and wire tool vendors will sell a variety of hand saws as well.

Bench Pin: When using a saw, a bench pin comes in handy because you can set the metal piece against it as you saw. This tool is useful for chain making as well as other metal work.

Saw Blades: Saw blades are necessary for a hand saw. The size of the blade used depends on the thickness of the material you plan to saw. For chain making, the necessary blade size ranges from size 2/0 to 2, with size 2/0 used for 20–22-gauge (0.9–0.65 mm) wire up to size 2 for 16–18-gauge (1.3–1 mm) wire. Blades come in packages of usually about a dozen.

Beeswax or Wax Compounds: A small amount of beeswax or a wax compound is used to coat saw blades in order to lubricate the blades before sawing.

Wire: Wire is the key ingredient to making jump rings. It takes a lot of jump rings to form a chain, depending on the complexity of the design, so a lot of wire is needed too. Round, square, and half-round wire are all useful for jump rings in gauges ranging from 20 to 14 (0.8 to 1.6 mm). When just starting out, consider using copper wire since it is softer and less expensive than silver wire. It is also nice to mix metals to create unusual-looking chain configurations.

Vise: A vise is an all-around useful tool. It will clamp onto mandrels and keep them in place when you wrap them with wire.

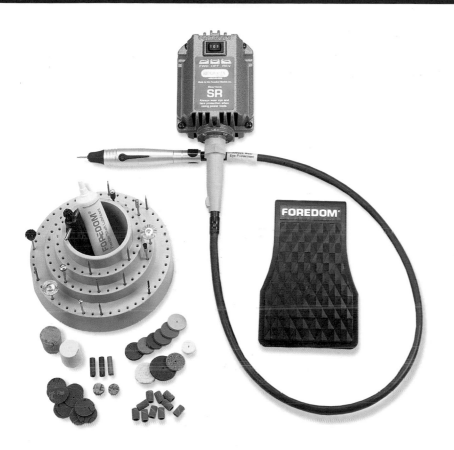

Jump Ringer: This trademarked system is composed of multiple pieces of equipment designed just for making many jump rings at one time. It includes mandrels in a variety of sizes, coil holder, and blades. To use this system, a rotary tool, which does not come with it, is also necessary. The rotary tool is used to power a saw blade to cut the jump rings after they are formed using the other pieces of equipment in system.

Techniques

This section describes a few different variations of jump ring making as well as how to connect the rings together once they are made. The method used often depends on how many rings are needed for a particular piece of jewelry.

FILING JUMP RINGS

Before learning to make jump rings, it is a good idea to have an understanding of how to file the rings after making them. An unsoldered jump ring has a cut across the ring. It is crucial that this cut is straight across the ring and perfectly smooth in order for the rings to properly close. Needle files are perfect for this purpose.

1 If the file doesn't fit through the cut in the jump ring, use chain-nose or flat-nose pliers—one pair in each hand—and grasp either side of the opening in the ring.

2 Open the jump ring by bringing one hand toward you and the other hand away from you at the same time. Do not pull the ring out from the sides. This will distort its shape.

3 Hold onto the open jump ring, and file across one side of the jump ring's opening with a needle file.

4 Do not file back and forth. Instead, file straight in one direction until that side is flat.

5 Repeat steps 3 and 4 for the other side of the jump ring's opening.

1

2

3

Tip

Remember to use heavy duty wire cutters when cutting thick gauges of wire, such as 16 gauge (1.3 mm) and larger.

WIRE CUTTER JUMP RINGS

If just a few jump rings are needed, this method of using wire cutters to cut off the rings is very quick and simple. It is also a good method for first-time jump ring makers.

1 Wrap the wire around a mandrel tightly so there are no spaces between each wrap. This will form a coil of wire around the mandrel.

2 Pull off the wire coil from the mandrel.

3 With wire cutters, cut individual rings from the coil.

4 Use needle files to smooth the cut areas of the rings using the Filing Jump Rings technique opposite.

2

3

1

4

JEWELER'S SAW JUMP RINGS

A jeweler's hand-saw will cut jump rings more precisely than a wire cutter will and may require very little to no filing afterward. This method is best for jewelry makers who are a little more advanced or who need a larger number of jump rings.

YOU WILL NEED

- wire of your choice
- mandrel
- needle file
- jeweler's saw
- saw blade
- beeswax or wax compound
- bench pin
- box or other container

1 Wrap the wire around a mandrel tightly so there are no spaces between each wrap to form a coil.

2 Pull the wire coil off the mandrel.

3 Take the saw and twist open the screws located on either side of saw opening.

4 Hold the saw blade so that the teeth on the blade are pointing down (not up) and out.

5 Take the wire coil (from step 2) and insert the blade through it.

6 With the coil around the blade, place the blade inside the open area of the saw with the ends of the blade under the screws.

7 Use your fingers to tighten each screw. Sometimes it is helpful to place the saw frame against the edge of a table or work bench to keep the saw steady, hold the handle, and push against the saw as you tighten the screws.

8 Test the blade's tension by gently pulling it with your fingers. It should make a high-pitched "ping" sound. If the blade is not tight enough, adjust it and tighten as necessary until the tension is right.

9 Rub a little beeswax or wax compound up and down the blade. Now you are ready to saw.

10 Place a box or other container under where you plan to saw. This will help catch the jump rings as they fall so that they don't scatter all over the floor.

2

5

9

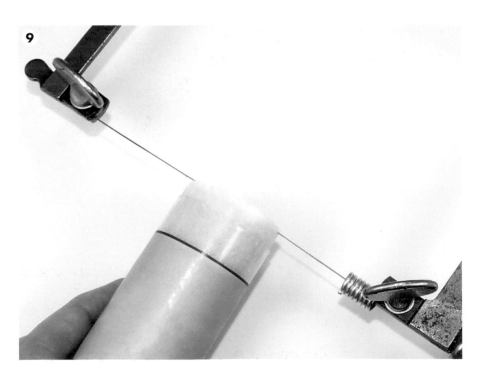

12

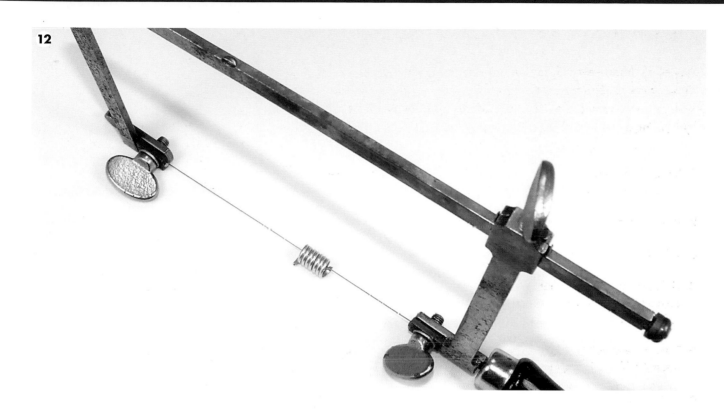

13

11 Grasp the jump rings with one hand and balance them over the open area of a bench pin. Conversely, because the bench pin is wood you can rest the full coil length on the bench pin.

12 With the other hand, grasp the handle of the saw and start sawing against the wire coil. Cutting happens on downward strokes, so keep an even and steady pace as you saw. Avoid gripping the saw handle too tightly or this may cause more of a jerking rather than a steady sawing motion.

13 As each ring is cut, it will fall through the bench pin opening. Holding the coil securely against the wooden bench pin, use even strokes to get a clean edge, cutting briefly into the bench pin. Collect and examine the rings to see if any need to be filed, and if so file them using the Filing Jump Rings technique on page 66.

Tip

Slow and steady is the best way to approach sawing. Going too fast makes the saw blades more likely to break.

JUMP RINGER TOOL

If you want to make a lot of jump rings and ensure that they are cut precisely, then the Jump Ringer combined with a rotary tool is an excellent choice. A fair amount of equipment is necessary, but for serious chain makers, serious tools are needed.

1 Select a mandrel for the size of jump rings you want to make, and insert it into the winder.

2 Tighten the chuck around the mandrel with the chuck key.

3 Stick one end of the wire into an opening in the winder, which is right above the mandrel.

4 Bend the wire a little, and while holding the wire, turn the handle of the winder around. As you do this, the wire will wrap around the mandrel creating a wire coil. Wrap the wire tightly around the mandrel.

5 Once you have the length of wire coil that you want, pull it off the mandrel, and use wire cutters to trim off any ends of wire that stick out.

6 Set the coil aside as you prepare the rotary tool for cutting.

7 Slip a blade guard on the end of the rotary tool that you hold with your hand.

8 Insert the blade into the end of the rotary tool, and tighten it down with the chuck ring.

9 Push the blade guard down to the end so that the opening on the guard lines up with the blade.

10 Place the blade guide over the opening and the blade to make sure the blade will line up in the middle of the blade guide. Once it is lined up, tighten the screw in the back of the blade guard so that the guide stays in place.

11 Now take the wire coil from step 6, slip it onto a wooden mandrel that is about same diameter or slightly smaller (sometimes a pencil works fine), and place it inside one of the coil holders. The wire coil should extend slightly above the top while it is in the coil holder.

12 Rub some beeswax over the wire coil.

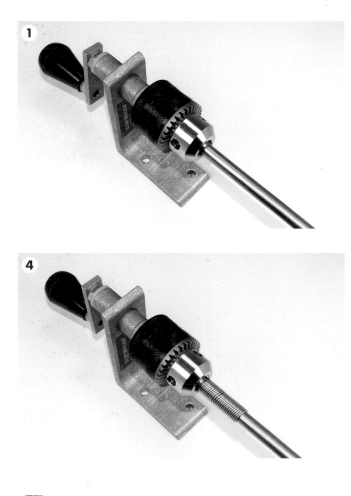

10

13

11

16

13 Take the cover of the coil holder, place it on top, and use the screws to secure it closed on top of the coil holder. Do not overtighten.

14 Take the rotary tool that you prepared in steps 7 to 10, turn it on, insert the blade in the track opening of the coil holder, and with an even swipe, push the blade guard down across the coil holder in one direction only while pressing on the rotary tool's pedal. Push the blade guard with a steady, even motion. Don't try to do it too quickly, or the rings could be damaged.

15 Take your foot off the pedal, allow the blade to stop turning, and pull the blade guard away from the coil holder.

16 Remove the cover of the coil holder, and empty out the jump rings.

CONNECTING JUMP RINGS

Quality jump rings are important to secure connections to each other or other jewelry components. The next step is to understand how to properly connect jump rings. There is a right way and a wrong way to open and close jump rings. The wrong way will distort the shape of the rings that you spent so much time making, and the rings will not stay closed very well either. The right way is literally a "snap" and means your jewelry pieces can handle lots of wear.

1   With a pair of chain-nose or flat-nose pliers in each hand, grasp either side of a jump ring.

2   Open the jump ring by bringing one hand toward you and the other hand away from you at the same time. Do not pull the ring out from the sides. This will distort its shape.

3   Slip a component or another jump ring onto the open jump ring, and again, hold either side of the jump ring with pliers in each hand.

4   To close the jump ring, bring one hand toward you and the other away until both ends of the jump ring meet. As the ends meet, they will "snap" together. You should actually hear them snap closed if you are doing it correctly.

YOU WILL NEED

- jump rings
- two chain-nose or flat-nose pliers

4

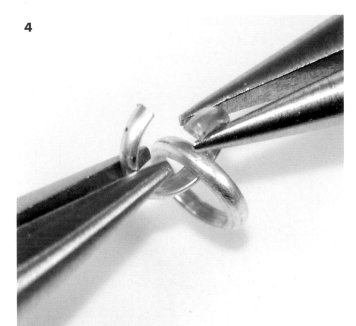

3

POLISHING AND TUMBLING

For many metal-based jewelry techniques, some cleaning and polishing of the metal is necessary. For chain making, it is a good idea to use a polisher to tumble finished chains. If beads or other items on the chains may be damaged by this, polish the chain jewelry piece in sections without any of the beads, and then complete the final assembly after each piece is polished. Polishing or tumbling will brighten up the chain as well as work harden all the jump rings that make up the chain. A magnetic polisher or tumbler is the preferred equipment to polish and tumble chains. These instructions demonstrate how to use a magnetic tumbler, but the same basic procedures can also be adapted for a rock tumbler. The primary difference is that a rock tumbler will take hours to do what a magnetic tumbler will do in a few minutes.

1. Start by putting the steel shot in the barrel of the polisher.

2. Add water up to the fill line, and squirt in a few drops of burnishing soap.

3. Place a chain (or other metal item that needs polishing) inside the barrel, and replace the lid.

4. Place the barrel on top of the magnetized base, and for an average-sized chain, turn the polisher's timer to 20 minutes and turn on the polisher. (If using a rock tumbler, set the chain to tumble for about two hours).

5. After the piece has finished tumbling, remove it and make sure it is clean enough. If it isn't as bright as you want it, use clean water and more burnishing soap and tumble the piece again until it has the desired brightness.

1

2

3

Tip

Some jewelry makers also use Dawn dish soap and a little lemon-scented ammonia instead of burnishing soap. Lemon-scented ammonia in addition to burnishing soap in the polisher also helps create a bright shine to metal pieces.

Projects

After making a large number of jump rings, the next step is to connect them and create some wonderful jewelry pieces. Any of the jump ring methods described in the techniques section can be used to make the jump rings for the following projects. Some additional techniques are also borrowed from the Wire Work section, page 40, in order to add extra elements such as pendants and clasps. Polishing requirements depend on how clean the wire is before you start working with it. Michael V. Powley contributed to the following chain-making projects.

DOUBLE UP TWO-TONE BRACELET

Add a little spice to a simple design by combining two kinds of metal: copper and silver. Each link of this chain is doubled up with two jump rings which then connect to two more jump rings, and so on. It is finished off with a lobster claw clasp. Dead-soft round wire was used to make the jump rings for this chain bracelet. The finished length, including the clasp, is 7 inches (17.8 cm).

YOU WILL NEED

- forty 5-mm sterling silver 16-gauge (1.3 mm) jump rings
- forty 5-mm copper 16-gauge (1.3 mm) jump rings
- one 3-mm sterling silver jump ring
- one 11-mm sterling silver lobster claw clasp
- two pairs of chain-nose pliers
- polisher and burnishing soap

3

5

7

1 With a pair of pliers in each hand, close two sterling silver jump rings.

2 Open one copper jump ring (page 72), and slip on the two silver jump rings from the previous step.

3 Close the copper jump ring around the two silver jump rings.

4 Slip a copper jump ring onto the other side of the two silver jump rings, and close the copper jump ring around the two silver jump rings.

5 Continue to connect two copper to two sterling jump rings alternating down the length of the chain until you have used all but one copper jump ring.

6 Take the 3-mm jump ring, and close it around the end of the clasp.

7 Using the last copper jump ring, open it up, and slip this onto the end of the chain and onto the jump ring attached to the clasp.

8 Close this last copper jump ring.

9 Run the bracelet through a polisher. Remove, rinse, and dry the bracelet.

10 To attach the bracelet to your wrist, connect the clasp to the jump ring on the opposite end of the chain (connected in step 2).

10

TWIST, SHOUT, AND DANGLE EARRINGS

Chains aren't meant to be used only as necklaces or bracelets. Graduated jump rings are made from twisted wire in these chain link earrings.

YOU WILL NEED

- four 3-mm 18-gauge (1 mm) half-hard sterling silver twisted wire jump rings
- four 5-mm half-hard sterling silver 16-gauge (1.3 mm) twisted wire jump rings
- four 8-mm half-hard sterling silver 16-gauge (1.3 mm) twisted wire jump rings
- two sterling silver ear hooks
- two pairs of chain-nose pliers
- polisher and burnishing soap

1 Using chain-nose pliers, connect one 5-mm jump ring and one 8-mm jump ring on either side of a 3-mm jump ring (page 72).

2 Repeat step 1 (A), but before closing the 3-mm jump ring, slip it around the 8-mm jump ring from the previous step (B).

3 Repeat steps 1 and 2 for the other jump rings.

4 Run the earring components through a polisher (page 73). Remove, rinse, and dry them.

5 Take a pair of ear hooks and make sure the hook's loops are oriented so that they are facing out rather than sideways. If necessary, use chain-nose pliers to twist the loops outward. ✷

6 Attach the top 3-mm jump ring of each wire component to the ear hook loops.

1

2A

2B

5

6

Tip

Twisted wire can be a little tricky to work with when closing jump rings. It will take a little extra manipulation with pliers.

COIL COPPER FLAME CHAIN

This chunky chain combines coils of 16-gauge (1.3 mm) round wire, formed using the process for making jump rings. The design was inspired by a similar technique used by Tim McCreight in his book, *Complete Metalsmith*. Instead of cutting individual links from the coil, simply cut out sections of coils, then connect them together with regular sterling jump rings. The final touch is a fused glass dichroic pendant that has the same bright copper effect as the wire on the chain. The finished length of the chain for this necklace is 20 inches (50.8 cm).

YOU WILL NEED

- thirty 4-mm half-hard sterling silver 18-gauge (1 mm) jump rings from half-round wire

- 90" (2.3 m) dead-soft copper 16-gauge (1.3 mm) wire

- 5-mm mandrel

- 24" (5 cm) sterling silver 16-gauge (1.3 mm) wire

- chain-nose pliers

- bent-nose pliers

- wire cutters

- pocket knife

- one dichroic fused glass pendant

- polisher and burnishing soap

1 Using any of the jump-ring-making techniques discussed previously in this section, make thirty 4-mm jump rings using 18-gauge (1.2 mm) sterling silver half-round wire. Set these aside for later.

2 Using 16-gauge (1.3 mm) copper wire and a 5-mm mandrel, make a long coil just as if you were going to make a lot of jump rings, but do not cut the rings.

3 Count over five wraps on the coil, and grasp this with bent-nose pliers.

4 Bend the wire coil at this point, and cut it off with wire cutters.

5 With chain-nose or bent-nose pliers, push the last wrap of the coil piece out and open to form a loop on the end of the wire coil piece.

6 Create another loop of wire on the other end of the coil piece by inserting the blade of a pocket knife between the last two wraps on the coil, and push this last wrap open.

7 You should have three wire wraps in the center of the wire piece with two loops of wire on each end. Repeat steps 3 to 6, making longer coils of wire as necessary, to make a total of 28 coiled sections.

8 Now start to connect the wire coil components with the sterling jump rings made in step 1 (A). Alternate between one copper coil and one sterling jump ring (B) until you have fourteen copper coils and thirteen jump rings connected.

8A

8B

2

5

14

15

9 Connect two more sterling jump rings to the last (number 14) copper coil.

10 Repeat steps 3 to 6 one time, but this time, count over three wraps on the coil instead of five.

11 Take the glass pendant, and snake it around the loops of this last wire coil component until it rests in the middle. Set this aside for later.

12 Repeat steps 2 to 9 to assemble the other side of the necklace, but leave the two chain sections separate at this point.

13 Take both chain sections, and run them through a polisher. Remove, rinse, and dry the chain sections.

14 Attach one side of the smaller coil made in step 10 to the two jump rings from step 9, and repeat this to connect the other side of the chain to the other side of the smaller coil section.

15 Use about 2" (5 cm) of 16-gauge (1.3 mm) sterling wire to make a hook clasp, and connect this to one end of the completed chain. (See Wire Work, page 48, for instructions on making a hook clasp).

16 Slip the hook around the loop on the end of the last copper coil to attach both ends of the necklace.

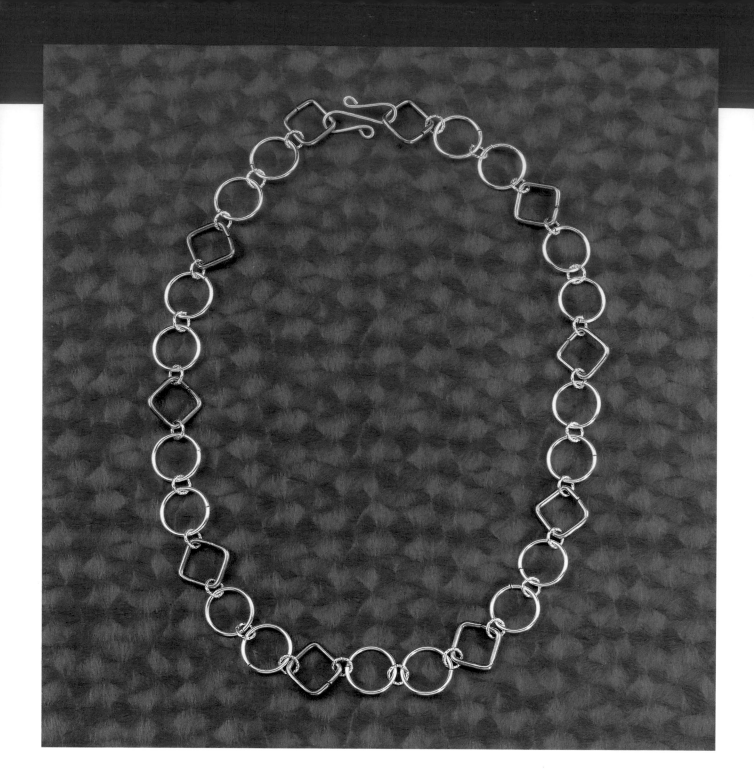

HIP SQUARES-VILLE CHAIN

Jump rings don't have to be round. Use a square mandrel to create the square-shaped jump rings. Unexpected combinations are always striking, so try mixing up jump ring shapes, sizes, colors, and textures. This 18-inch (45.7 cm) chain is a mix of large round, large square, and smaller twisted round links. The metals used include sterling silver and brass that has an antique finish.

YOU WILL NEED

- ten 11-mm square-shaped brass 16-gauge (1.3 mm) jump rings

- eighteen 12-mm round-shaped sterling silver 18-gauge (1 mm) jump rings

- twenty-seven 3-mm sterling silver twisted wire 18-gauge (1 mm) jump rings

- 2½" (6.4 cm) sterling silver 18-gauge (1 mm) wire

- two pairs of chain-nose pliers

- round-nose pliers

- wire cutters

- polisher and burnishing soap

1 Use 18-gauge (1 mm) wire and make an S-shaped hook using Wire Hook instructions (page 48), but instead of forming a hook on one side and a curl on the opposite end of the hook, form a hook on both sides of the wire. This creates the S shape of the hook. Set this aside for later.

2 Connect the following jump rings together: one square jump ring, one small twisted wire jump ring, one large round jump ring, one small twisted wire jump ring, one large round jump ring, and one small twisted wire jump ring.

3 Repeat step 2 using the rest of the jump rings and make sure to end with a square jump ring.

4 Run the chain through a polisher. Remove, rinse, and dry it.

5 Connect both ends of the chain by slipping them onto the S-shaped clasp created in step 1.

1

3

2

5

RED RHAPSODY DOUBLE CHAIN BRACELET

Create a basic link chain and then a chain made from links and beads for this dramatic double strand bracelet. Both strands connect to a silver toggle clasp. The Unwrapped Loop from page 46 is used for the bead and jump ring chain.

YOU WILL NEED

- thirty-seven 5-mm sterling silver 18-gauge (1 mm) jump rings
- 24" (61 cm) sterling silver 21-gauge (0.7 mm) wire
- nine 6-mm Swarovski Siam red crystal beads
- one 13-mm sterling silver toggle clasp
- two pairs of chain-nose pliers
- round-nose pliers
- wire cutters
- polisher and burnishing soap

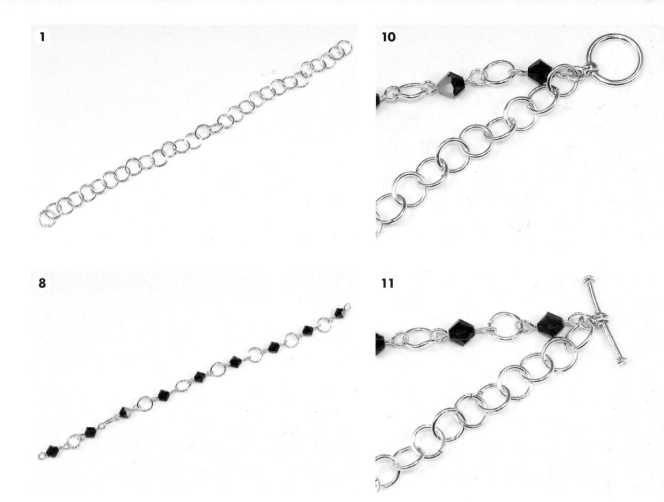

1 Using two pairs of chain-nose pliers, connect twenty-nine jump rings together. Set this chain aside for later.

2 Take 21-gauge (0.7 mm) wire and, using the Unwrapped Loop instructions (page 46), make an unwrapped loop on the end of the wire.

3 Slip on a crystal bead, and finish the other end of the wire with another unwrapped loop.

4 Repeat step 2 and 3 until you have nine wire bead pieces.

5 Take eight jump rings, and close each one using chain-nose pliers.

6 Run the jump rings just closed and the chain made in step 1 through a polisher. Remove, rinse, and dry them.

7 Next, connect one unwrapped loop from a wire and bead piece to one of the jump rings from step 5.

8 Connect another bead and wire piece to this jump ring, and continue alternating bead sections and jump rings until all nine bead and wire sections and jump rings are used. There should be a bead and wire section on each end of this piece.

9 Take the chain made in step 1, open a jump ring on one end, slip it onto one side of the toggle clasp, and close the jump ring.

10 Take the bead and jump ring chain made in steps 2–8, use chain-nose pliers to open the unwrapped loop on the end, slip this onto one side of the toggle clasp, and close the loop.

11 Repeat steps 9 to 10 for the other side of the bracelet and toggle clasp.

METAL FABRICATION

Turning sheets of metal and rolls of wire into jewelry components using hand tools and no soldering is called metal fabrication. Metal fabrication techniques prepare metal pieces for the soldering process, but there is still a lot of interesting jewelry to be made by exclusively using fabrication techniques. Like any type of jewelry making, it takes practice, but the basics are not that difficult to master. It can also be a lot of fun as you pound, stamp, and bend metal to your will.

Tools and Supplies

Along with standard jewelry tools such as chain-nose pliers (see General Jewelry-Making Tools on page 9), tools used for wire work and chain making are also used for fabrication. In a way, fabrication actually encompasses wire manipulation, so it makes sense that many of the tools and supplies will cross over. Wire working and chain making tools that you will also need for fabrication include the following: rawhide hammer, anvil or bench block, rotary tool, jeweler's saw, saw blades, beeswax or wax compound, bench pin, and polishing tumbler. However, in addition to these tools there are some other tools useful for fabrication, especially when working with metal sheet.

Assortment of Hammers: An assortment of hammers is helpful for forming, flattening, and texturing metal including a chasing hammer, ball-peen hammer, and a rawhide mallet. A chasing hammer has a large flat area on one side and round area on the other. The flat side is used for striking chasing tools, such as marking stamps. The round side of a chasing hammer is similar to a ball-peen hammer, so it is useful for texturing. A ball-peen hammer is used for shaping, flattening, and texturing. One side is round (like a ball), and the other side is flat. Though this side of the hammer isn't as large as a chasing hammer, it can also be used with marking stamps. Finally, a rawhide hammer or mallet helps form, bend, and flatten metal without marking or scratching it.

Mandrels: Mandrels are necessary in order to shape the metal when making bracelets and rings from metal sheets and wire. They come in lots of different sizes and shapes. Most are made from heavy steel, though wood mandrels are also available.

Large Files: Large files are useful for working with large metal sheets. They are made of steel and have a broad work surface, so they can cover more area when filing.

Metal Stamps: Decorate metal with lettering or fun symbols by using metal stamps. The stamp shanks are made from high-carbon steel. Buy them separately or in sets.

Burnisher: Most burnishing tools have a wooden handle attached to a pointed piece of steel. Jewelers use this tool to push metal areas into place to form prongs or bezels.

Hole Punch: Light-gauge metals (24-gauge [0.5 mm] or less) can be easily punched by this handy little tool. It has two hole sizes, 1.5 mm and 2 mm.

Drill Press (not shown): Just about any hardware store will carry some type of drill press tool. These are used for drilling holes through all kinds of materials, from wood to metal. The drill is secured to a stand, and a handle is used to lower the drill bit down and into the material.

Metal Shears: These look like very large scissors. They are made out of tempered steel and are designed to cut metal sheet.

Glue (not shown): Rubber cement or a glue stick is used to attach paper templates to metal plate before cutting out shapes.

Templates: Draftsmen use these same kinds of templates, but for jewelry makers, these are useful for cutting out geometric metal shapes.

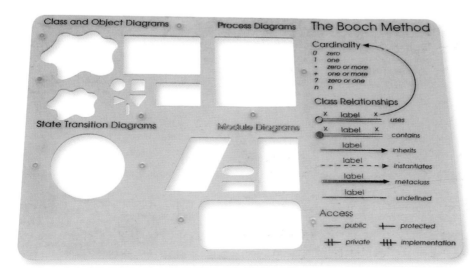

Techniques

This section covers the foundational methods used for fabricating metal. Sawing, filing, and forming are the fundamentals of metal working, so most beginners start with these methods before moving onto more advanced techniques.

METAL HOLES

Metal pieces, such as pendants or earring components, will often require holes so they can connect to other jewelry pieces including ear wires, jump rings, clasps, and bails. There are different ways to make a hole in a metal piece depending on its thickness. For sheet that is 24-gauge (0.5 mm) or thinner, a simple metal hole punch tool will usually work. For a metal sheet that is thicker than 24 gauge (0.5 mm), use a drill.

Using a Hole Punch Tool

1 To use a hole punch tool, first determine where you want the hole in your metal to be located and mark it with an X.

2 Position the X inside the hole punch (on either end of the tool depending on whether the hole should be 1.5 or 2 mm).

3 Turn the hole punch handle until it pierces a hole through the sheet.

YOU WILL NEED

- metal sheet
- hole punch
- marker

2

Using a Rotary Tool or Drill Press

YOU WILL NEED

- metal sheet
- rotary tool or drill press
- nail
- block of wood
- pliers

1 Place the metal piece over a block of wood.

2 Determine where you want the hole in your metal to be located, place the nail on the spot for the hole, and use a hammer to hit the nail a few times. This will dent the metal but not put a hole in it.

3 Use pliers to hold the metal in place and with either the rotary tool or drill press, bring the drill bit down onto the dent marked in the previous step.

4 Drill until the bit pierces the metal and just hits the block of wood.

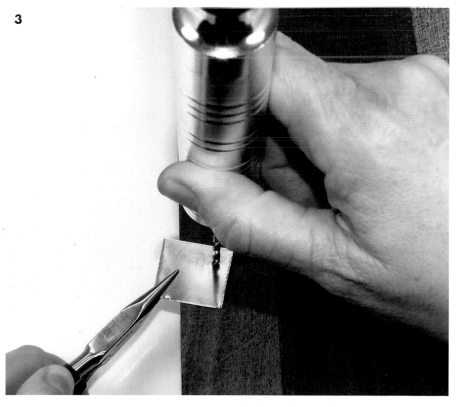

SAWING METAL

Use a jeweler's saw to cut metal sheet or wire. In addition to the saw, saw blades and beeswax or a wax compound is necessary.

YOU WILL NEED

- metal sheet
- jeweler's saw
- saw blades
- beeswax or wax compound
- bench pin

1 Make sure the saw blade teeth on the blade are pointing down (not up) and out.

2 Place the blade inside the open area of the saw with the ends of the blade under the screws.

3 Tighten each screw to secure the blade inside the saw. Sometimes it is helpful to place the saw frame against the edge of a table or work bench to keep the saw steady, hold the handle, and push against the saw as you tighten the screws.

4 Gently pull on the blade with your fingers to test the blade's tension. It should make a high-pitched "ping" sound. If the blade is not tight enough, adjust it and tighten as necessary until the tension is right.

5 Rub some wax compound up and down the blade.

6 Grasp the metal item, such as metal sheet, with one hand and balance it horizontally over either the side of a table or preferably a bench pin.

7 With the other hand, grasp the handle of the saw and start sawing at a slight right angle against the metal, keeping an even and steady pace as cutting happens on downward strokes. Avoid gripping the saw handle too tightly or this may cause more of a jerking rather than a steady sawing motion.

Tip

It may be necessary to add more beeswax or wax compound periodically during sawing depending on the size of the metal piece.

PIERCING METAL

This technique provides a way to work within, or in the center of, a metal piece instead of just cutting it from the outside. Holes are pierced in the metal sheet, providing a starting place for cutting the metal.

YOU WILL NEED

- metal sheet
- hole punch, rotary tool, or drill press
- jeweler's saw
- saw blades
- beeswax or wax compound

1 Use one of the metal hole cutting techniques on page 88 to cut a hole through the metal in the area you want to start sawing.

2 Take a saw blade, coat it with wax, and secure one end of it into the saw.

3 Snake the other end of the blade through the hole created in step 1, and then secure that end into the saw.

4 Cut out the area desired inside of the metal piece, adding more wax on the blade as necessary.

5 When finished, simply unscrew one end of the saw to loosen one end of the blade, and pull the blade and saw from the metal piece. Depending on the design being cut from the metal, it may be necessary to pierce the metal and insert the saw blade and saw numerous times as you move around inside of the metal piece.

FILING METAL

Filing metal helps to smooth out rough areas and remove scratches and other imperfections in the metal that might occur while working with it. For fabrication of metal sheet and wire, both large files and smaller needle files are usually necessary depending on the jewelry piece being formed. Large files are used for large surfaces, while needle files are useful for nooks and crannies.

YOU WILL NEED

- metal of choice
- file of choice
- bench pin (optional)

1 Grasp the metal item in one hand and the file in the other. (For very large pieces of metal it is helpful to balance the metal against a bench pin while working.)

2 Push the face of the file against the metal piece and away from you in one even stroke.

3 After making one sweep against the metal piece with the file, pull up with the file and start again, continuing to work in one direction rather than back and forth.

4 Check the metal piece to see if it is smooth or needs more filing, and continue to file as necessary until the desired smoothness is achieved.

TEXTURING METAL

Texturing metal sheets is simple and creates another design element for finished jewelry pieces. While there are lots of different methods for texturing metal, one of the simplest is to use a hammer.

YOU WILL NEED

- metal of choice
- ball-peen hammer
- anvil

1 Place the metal piece on top of the anvil, and hold it in place with one hand.

2 Grasp the hammer with the other hand, and start pounding against the metal using the "ball" side of the hammer.

3 Make sure to cover the entire piece if you want all of it textured.

4 Try to use the same force for each blow of the hammer so that the pattern created will look uniform.

2

FORGING METAL AROUND MANDRELS

Whenever metal is moved by force, this is considered a type of forging. For example, as a way to form jewelry pieces such as rings and bracelets, metal pieces are formed or forged around mandrels, thus aiding in shaping the metal piece.

YOU WILL NEED

- metal of choice
- rawhide hammer
- mandrel of choice

1 Wrap the metal piece (wire or sheet) around the mandrel, and hold it in place.

2 Take a rawhide hammer, and while holding the metal piece, tap the hammer against the metal and mandrel.

1

Tip

When practicing new metal techniques, one way to save on the cost of materials is to use more economic metals such as brass or copper before trying them with higher end metals such as gold and silver.

3 Continue to tap using as much force as necessary to form the metal around the mandrel. Thinner gauge and softer metal will take less force than thicker and harder metal pieces.

4 The metal piece may need to be adjusted or moved around on the mandrel depending on the jewelry piece being formed, but continue to tap with the hammer until the desired shape of metal is achieved.

Tip

If the metal becomes hard and brittle while forging and is almost impossible to bend any longer, consider annealing it. This requires heating the metal with a torch until the metal turns red and then leaving it to cool before working with it again. Some jewelers will quench (put the hot metal in cold water to cool it quickly); however, too often this ends up making the metal piece too hard to work with again, so it is best to let it cool on its own.

METAL STAMPING

One way to personalize a metal jewelry piece is to use metal stamps. There are many ways to use these stamps, from adding initials to creating simple ornamental elements. While this technique is not difficult, it does take some practice. It is a good idea to practice on scrap sheet before stamping on an almost finished jewelry piece.

2

3

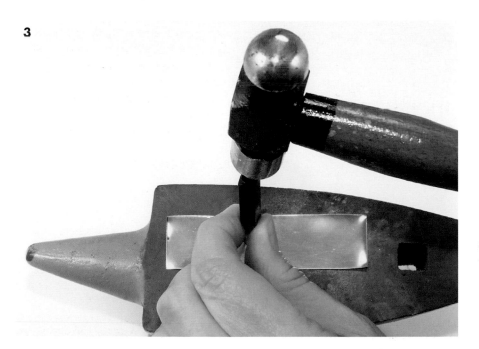

1 Place the metal piece on an anvil, and determine where the stamped letters, numbers, or symbols should be located. (A marker and ruler can be helpful to mark these areas on the metal.)

2 With one hand, hold the first stamp in place.

3 With the other hand, use the flat part of a ball-peen hammer or a chasing hammer and hit the top of the stamp. (For a less forceful hit, hold the handle of the hammer closer to the hammer's head.)

Projects

From earrings to bracelets and necklaces, use fabrication skills to construct any number of jewelry pieces without the need for solder. These five projects are a good jumping-off point for any beginning metal worker.

HAMMER IT OUT TEXTURED EARRINGS

Though cutting metal sheet with a jeweler's saw is usually best, it is also possible to cut thin metal sheet with metal cutting shears. The difference is that cutting with shears can bend the sheet, sometimes making it necessary to flatten the cut-out metal piece. This geometric earring project uses metal shears to cut the metal, but a saw is also fine to use. Other techniques used include Piercing, Filing, and Hammering.

YOU WILL NEED

- 2" (5 cm) of 24-gauge (0.5 mm) brass sheet
- 4" to 5" (10.2 to 12.7cm) of 21-gauge (0.7 mm) brass wire
- metal cutting shears
- large file
- needle file
- ball-peen hammer
- rawhide hammer
- anvil
- hole punch
- ruler
- marker
- polishing cloth
- chain-nose pliers
- wire cutter
- round-nose pliers

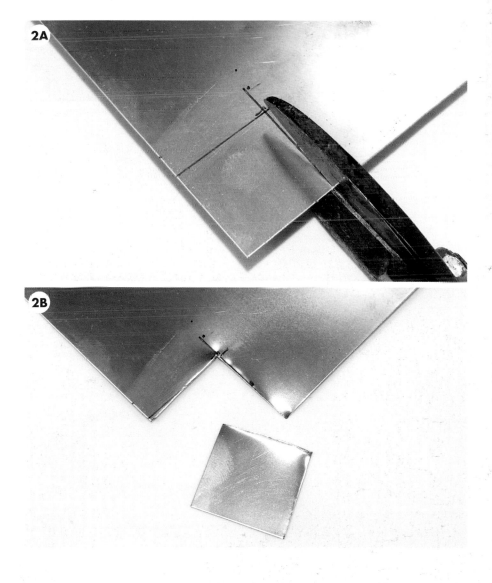

1 Mark a 1" (2.5 cm) square on the sheet. (One trick to cutting less is to start marking off the area on the corner of the sheet. This way, only two cuts are required, rather than four.)

2 Following the lines drawn in step 1 (A), use metal shears to cut out the square (B).

(continued)

3 With a ruler, locate the top/center of the square, and use the marker to mark this spot with a large X.

4 Position the X inside the hole punch, and turn the hole punch handle until it pierces a hole through the sheet.

5 Use a large file to file all sides of the square cut by the shears.

6 Place the 1" (2.5 cm) brass square on an anvil and texture it with a ball-peen hammer all over one side.

7 Place the brass square on an anvil, and use a rawhide hammer to flatten the piece. It may be necessary to flip the sheet over and pound the other side as well.

8 Clean off all fingerprints and any leftover marker ink with a polishing cloth.

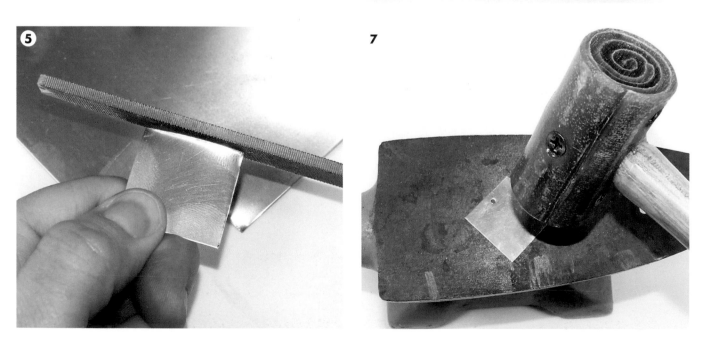

10

12

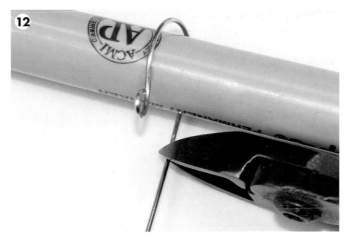

11

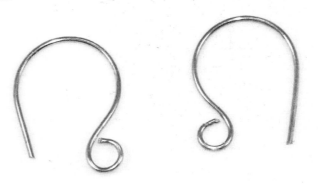

13

9 Repeat all the steps above to create a second textured brass square component, and set these aside for later.

10 Take the brass wire, and use round-nose pliers to form a small loop on one end.

11 With the loop facing outward, hold the straight part of the wire against the marker previously used, and with your fingers, wrap the wire 180 degrees (halfway) around the marker.

12 Trim off excess wire just past the marker, and file the wire end with a needle nose file until it is smooth.

13 Repeat steps 10 to 12 to create another ear hook.

14 Use chain-nose pliers to open the loops on each ear hook a little, slip the loops onto the holes of each brass square component, and close the ear hook loops.

Tip

The more a piece of metal is manipulated the harder it will become. This is referred to as work hardening, see page 92.

KOKOPELLI COIN PENDANT

Precious metal coins are the perfect size for creating a variety of jewelry designs. This pendant project starts with a silver half dollar. With the aid of piercing and filing, it is transformed into a southwestern-style pendant. While the Kokopelli figure is used for this pendant project, any number of designs can be cut into the center of the coin.

YOU WILL NEED

- one silver half-dollar coin
- 5-mm sterling silver jump ring
- computer, printer, and paper
- Kokopelli image
- glue stick
- scissors
- rotary tool or drill press
- large file
- needle file
- jeweler's saw
- saw blades
- beeswax or wax compound
- chain-nose pliers

1 Take a large file and file the "head" side of the coin so that it is blank. This will leave the "tail" side, or the side with the eagle on it.

2 Use an online search engine to locate a Kokopelli image, size it if necessary, and print it out.

1

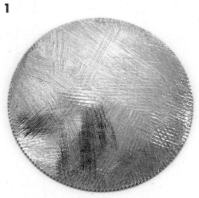

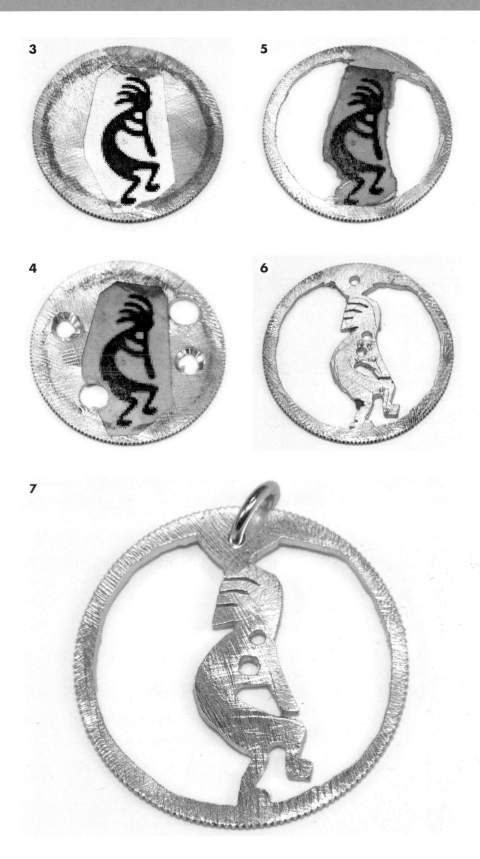

3 Cut out the paper image, cover the back with glue, and paste it onto the blank side of the coin created in step 1.

4 Use a drill press or rotary tool and cut out four holes, two on either side of the image.

5 Using the piercing technique, insert the blade of the saw through one hole and start sawing the larger areas of metal to be removed around the image. At this point, don't worry about getting the details of the image sawed out. The idea is to remove the silver on either side.

6 Now that the metal on either side of the image has been removed, it will be easier to move the saw around. Using the piercing technique, now work on cutting directly around the image to form the details of the Kokopelli.

7 Use a drill press or rotary tool to drill a hole through the top of the coin, and add a jump ring.

8 File around the inside of the coin and around the image with a needle file. This will help remove scratches and also define the image.

9 Polish in either a tumbler or with the rotary tool. (See the Chain Making section, page 73, for polishing techniques).

SUBSTANTIALLY SILVER CUFF BRACELET

Though the look is big and bold, this textured cuff bracelet is actually very lightweight and comfortable to wear since it is made using 18-gauge (1 mm) sterling silver sheet. Techniques used include Sawing, Forging, Filing, and Texturing.

YOU WILL NEED

- ½" (1.3 cm) wide 18-gauge (1 mm) sterling silver sheet
- round bracelet mandrel
- large file
- jeweler's saw
- saw blades
- beeswax or wax compound
- ball-peen hammer
- rawhide hammer
- anvil
- marker
- ruler
- polisher

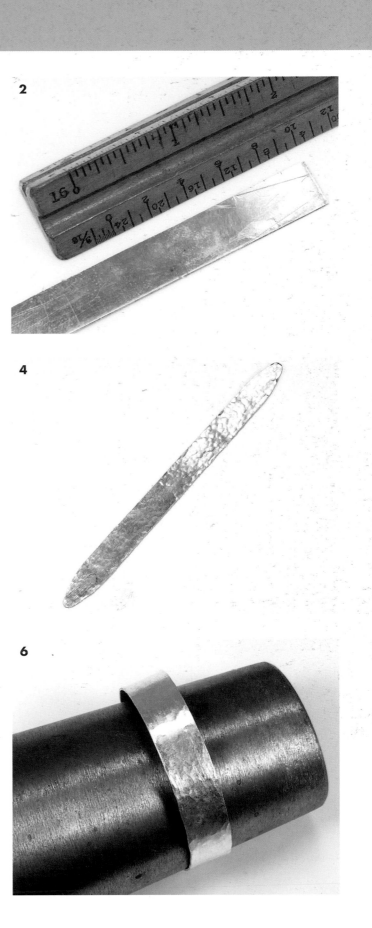

1 Start by using a saw (page 90) to cut a piece from the metal sheet that it is ½" (1.3 cm) wide and 6" (15 cm) long.

2 Use a ruler to measure and mark off the corners of the piece, and then saw them off to help taper both ends.

3 File the cut areas using a large file (page 91).

4 Place the silver piece on an anvil and texture it with a ball-peen hammer (page 92).

5 Bend the piece around the round bracelet mandrel (page 92).

6 Holding the piece around the mandrel, pound it with a rawhide hammer all around the mandrel.

7 Remove the bracelet from the mandrel, polish it, and it is ready to wear.

Tip

Fishing tackle boxes work really well for storing and transporting jewelry tools.

STERLING AND GARNET PADDLE PIECE NECKLACE

This project combines fabrication techniques with a little wire work and some gorgeous faceted garnet beads. The fabricated paddle pieces in this necklace have lots of design possibilities.

3

4

YOU WILL NEED

- 7½" (19 cm) of 18-gauge (1 mm) half-hard sterling silver round wire
- 6" (15 cm) of 24-gauge (0.5 mm) dead-soft sterling silver round wire
- 2" (5 cm) of 21-gauge (0.7 mm) dead-soft sterling round wire
- two sterling chain pieces 7½" (19 cm) long
- one 5-mm sterling jump ring
- eight 4-mm facet garnet beads
- needle file
- chasing or ball-peen hammer
- rawhide hammer
- anvil
- ruler
- polishing cloth
- chain-nose pliers
- round-nose pliers

1 Take the 18-gauge (1 mm) wire, grasp it with a polishing cloth, and pull it through the cloth a few times to shine it a little.

2 Cut a 1½" (3.8 cm) piece of 18-gauge (1 mm) wire, and file both ends with a needle file.

3 Use a pair of round-nose pliers to curl one end of the wire.

4 With a pair of chain-nosed pliers, hold the wire on an anvil, making sure the curl faces down.

(continued)

5 Use a chasing hammer or the flat side of a ball-peen hammer to flatten the wire.

6 Cut more of the 18-gauge (1 mm) wire into sections as follows: two 1¼" (3.2 cm) pieces; two 1" (2.5 cm) pieces; and two ¾" (1.9 cm) pieces.

7 Repeat steps 3 to 5 using the wire sections cut in step 6. At this point, there should be a total of seven paddle pieces.

8 Use a polishing cloth to polish each paddle piece again. (If the wire is considerably tarnished, consider using a polisher at this point before continuing.)

9 With the 24-gauge (0.5 mm) wire, chain-nose, and round-nose pliers, make a wrapped loop (see Wire Work, page 47) on one end of the wire, but before closing up the wire, slip the end of one chain piece onto the loop.

5

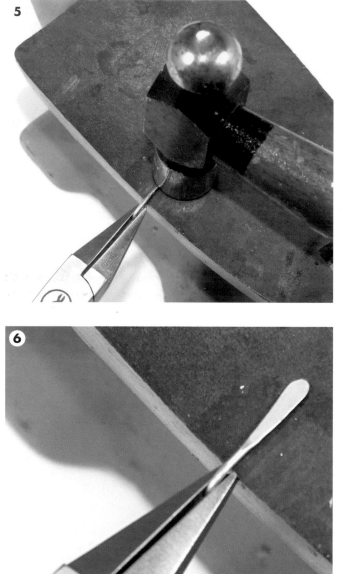

7

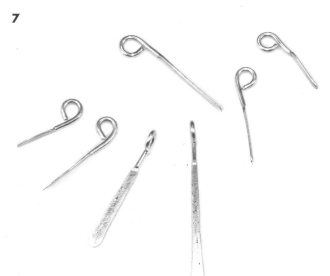

6

9

10

10 Starting with a garnet bead, alternately thread the paddle pieces and garnet beads onto the wire starting with the smaller paddle piece, then moving up in size until the longest piece is in the center, and then moving back down to the smaller sized paddle pieces.

11 Make another wrapped loop on the end of the wire and connect the other chain section to this loop before wrapping it closed.

12 Attach a jump ring on one end of the chain.

13 Make a wire hook using the 21-gauge (0.7 mm) wire (see Wire Work, page 48), and finish the necklace by attaching this to the other side of the chain.

Tip

If you have dogs, remember to keep tools like rawhide hammers away so that they don't become a big chew toy.

YOU WILL NEED

- 1" × 1" (2.5 × 2.5 cm) of sterling silver 16-gauge (1.3 mm) sheet
- 2" (5 cm) of 16-gauge (1.3 mm) dead-soft copper wire
- computer, printer, and paper
- heart image
- glue stick
- scissors
- rotary tool or drill press
- large file
- needle files
- jeweler's saw
- saw blades
- beeswax or wax compound
- ball-peen or chasing hammer
- ring mandrel
- rawhide hammer
- anvil
- X and O metal stamps
- two 5-mm sterling silver jump rings
- one 3-mm sterling silver jump ring
- chain-nose pliers
- polisher
- liver of sulfur
- baking soda
- two small bowls of water
- tweezers
- paper towels
- microwave
- polishing cloth

SHOT THROUGH THE HEART PENDANT

A copper arrow pierces a sterling silver heart in this fun pendant project that combines a number of fabrication techniques: Sawing, Filing, Stamping, and Making Holes. The letters X and O from the stamp set represent hugs and kisses that are scattered over the front of the sterling heart.

1 Use a computer and printer to print out a heart shape that is about 1" × 1" (2.5 × 2.5 cm) After printing the heart, cut out the paper shape with scissors.

2 Use a glue stick to coat the back of the paper heart and adhere it to a piece of sterling sheet.

(continued)

2

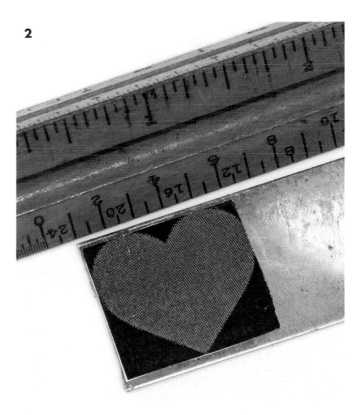

3 With a jeweler's saw, saw around the heart.

4 Use large and needle nose files to file all around the heart to ensure the sides are smooth.

5 Pierce a hole in the top/center area of the heart and pierce two extra holes across the heart that will later hold the copper arrow.

6 Using an X and an O metal stamp as well as an anvil and hammer, stamp in various spots across the silver heart.

7 To create a little bit of a curve in the metal sheet, hold the heart against the widest area of a ring mandrel and use a rawhide hammer to mold the heart around it.

8 Take a few inches (centimeters) of copper wire, and insert it through the two holes created in step 5.

9 Use a hammer and anvil to flatten both ends of the copper wire (while it is still inserted into the silver heart).

10 With a needle file, shape one end of the wire into the arrow point and the other end the feathers.

3A

4A

6

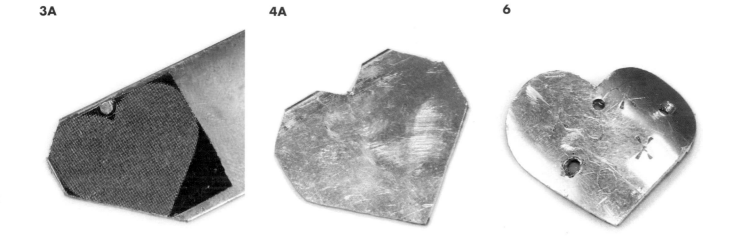

3B

4B

8

11 Attach a 5-mm jump ring to the center hole in the heart, then add a 3-mm jump ring, and another 5-mm jump ring so that there are three jump rings attached to the center hole.

12 Polish the heart either in a tumbler or with the rotary tool. (See the Chain Making section, page 73, for polishing techniques). If you prefer the pendant polished, skip the last few steps of this project. To give it a patina, which will help the X and O stamping show up a little more, continue.

13 Fill two small bowls with water, and microwave one bowl for about 60 seconds. It should be warm, but not boiling.

14 Take a small chunk of liver of sulfur, set it in the warm bowl of water, and use tweezers to stir the water a little. It is harmless but will start to smell like rotten eggs, so it is a good idea to work in a well-ventilated area.

15 Sprinkle about a tablespoon of baking soda in the other bowl of water.

16 Place the heart pendant in the liver of sulfur water, use tweezers to pull it out after a few seconds, and place in the bowl with the water and baking soda. (The baking soda neutralizes the affects of the liver of sulfur.)

17 Pull out the pendant, dry it off with a paper towel. If it has the look you want, you are finished. If you want to remove some of the patina, rub it with a polishing cloth. If you want it darker, repeat step 16 until it has the look you desire.

METAL SOLDERING

Solder is a metal alloy. Soldering is the method used to melt solder so that it flows in between metal joints, ultimately connecting them. Some beginning jewelry makers are hesitant at first to attempt soldering since it requires the use of a torch; however, with practice, it is easy to master. Plus, having the ability to permanently join metals together brings with it a great deal of creative power. Practice regularly, follow some basic rules, and be prepared to learn from mistakes. These are the elements needed to solder successfully.

Tools and Supplies

Along with many of the same tools used for metal fabrication (such as files, hammers, and saws) and general hand tools (such as pliers and wire cutters), soldering requires some specialized pieces of equipment. Jewelry supply vendors carry many of these items, and for the most part, it is possible to get started with a fairly low investment. (See Jewelry Supply Resources, page 290, for vendors who sell many of the supplies described below.)

Torch: The torch is one of the first tools to consider. Usually butane, propane, and acetylene are the fuels used for soldering. Butane is the same liquid gas used in cigarette lighters, so it is easily available. A small hand-held butane torch is a good choice for beginners, and it is also very portable. Propane is another fuel that is easy to obtain as most hardware stores carry various sizes of propane tanks. A torch attachment such as a pencil torch kit attaches to the top of the tank. Like the butane torch, this option is good for hobbyist or beginners due to portability and cost. For more experienced or professional jewelers who plan to do a lot of soldering, the choice is frequently a torch connected to an acetylene tank, which is a great deal larger than an average propane tank.

Solder: Solder comes in sheet or wire form, and there are various grades available depending on the type of metal being soldered. Three types are the most common, particularly when soldering silver: hard, medium, and soft, and they are normally used in order starting from the hardest solder, which also has the highest melting point. Because each of these solders melt at different temperatures, this regulates when they are used. Hard silver solder (with a melting point of 1425°F [773°C]) is used when first soldering a piece. As more soldering is required on a piece, work down to the lower-temperature melting solders. Use medium silver solder (with a melting point of 1390°F [747°C]) for secondary soldering. Easy silver solder (with a melting point of 1325°F [711 °C]) is used at the end of the soldering process or if only one soldering is required. For other metals, such as gold and copper, there are specific solders available as well; however, for gold, lower karat gold can be used as solder. So 10-kt gold works as solder for 14-kt gold, 14-kt gold solders 18-kt gold, and so on.

Soldering Pad: To protect the soldering area, a protective, heat-resistant pad is necessary. There are a number of surfaces available from asbestos-free pads to charcoal blocks. The flame from the torch will scar and discolor the surface, but they are still fine to use.

Pickle and Pickle Pot: It is critical to keep metals clean and free from oils when soldering, so an acidic solution is required to clean metal pieces before soldering. This solution is referred to as "pickle" and must be stored in a safe container, called a "pickle pot." This small crock pot with its ceramic inner bowl works well. Liquid or powder solutions are available for mixing pickle and are normally diluted with water.

Copper Tongs: To place and remove metal pieces inside a pickle pot, copper tongs are required because they will not react to the pickle solution. Other metal will contaminate the solution and the metal placed inside the pickling agent.

Torch Striker: Used to light the flame on a torch, a torch striker has a small piece of flint that ignites a spark when the handle is pulled and released.

Shop Shears: Only a tiny amount of solder is required for each joint, so shop shears are helpful when cutting either wire solder or sheet solder.

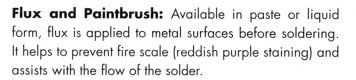

Flux and Paintbrush: Available in paste or liquid form, flux is applied to metal surfaces before soldering. It helps to prevent fire scale (reddish purple staining) and assists with the flow of the solder.

Third Hand: Just as the name implies, sometimes a third hand can help when soldering, and that is exactly how this piece of equipment works. Use the jaws to hold an item in place and have both hands free to solder.

Soldering Tripod and Screen: When it is necessary to solder a piece of metal from underneath, a metal tripod covered by a piece of heavy-duty heating screen is preferable to use as a soldering surface. This allows for even heating from all sides while moving the torch around.

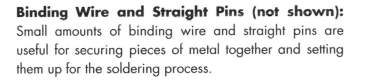

Binding Wire and Straight Pins (not shown): Small amounts of binding wire and straight pins are useful for securing pieces of metal together and setting them up for the soldering process.

Glass Jar (not shown): Recycle a glass jar and use it to hold water for quenching metal.

Tweezers: Tweezers are useful for placing tiny amounts of solder.

Techniques

The soldering techniques discussed in this section cover many of the basics required to complete a successful soldering procedure, from cleaning the metal with pickling solution to the actual heating of the metal with a torch. While the rules for soldering properly are pretty much the same, the actual methods can vary from one jeweler to another depending on personal choice and comfort levels. For example, some jewelers prefer to hold the torch in one hand and a probe in the other, applying the solder with the probe and then soldering directly afterward; however, other jewelers prefer the more traditional "chip" method (described in this section) where tiny chips of solder are strategically placed before turning on the torch. After learning this standard technique, you can experiment with the way the solder and flame are applied, as long as the basic soldering rules are followed.

Tip

Before attempting any type of soldering, it is important to follow some safety precautions. Keep hair pulled back, and make sure sleeves or other clothing items are not in the way while working. Remove any materials from the work area that may be flammable such as paper or plastic. Fuel tanks should be secured and their fittings correctly attached. Work in a well-ventilated area, and wear protective safety gear when working with pickle and other acidic materials.

PICKLING METAL

Before starting to solder, a pickling solution must first be mixed together so that metal pieces can be thoroughly cleaned.

1 Any number of pickling solutions can be used for pickling. Follow the manufacturer's instructions for diluting with water, and remember to wear safety gear (goggles, apron, gloves) while mixing.

YOU WILL NEED

- pickling solution
- slow cooker
- copper tongs
- electrical outlet
- safety gear

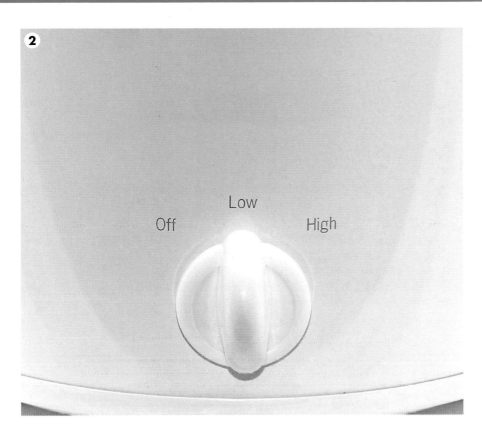

2 Store the mixture in a slow cooker dedicated for metal pickling only. This pot should never be used again for food products.

3 Turn the slow cooker on low, and use copper tongs to stir and ensure the solution dissolves properly.

4 Pick up metal pieces with tongs, and place inside the heated pickle pot. Do not drop them in, as this may cause the acid solution to splash up.

5 Keep the metal item in the pickle for 3 to 5 minutes depending on the size of the piece.

6 When clean, use copper tongs to remove the metal piece, and wash the piece under running water. (It is also a good idea to wash your hands with soap and water at this point.)

7 Use this pickling procedure before each soldering attempt to ensure metal pieces are clean of loose oxides and flux. For multi-step projects, make sure to first remove any binding wire that may have been used while soldering.

CUTTING SOLDER

A little solder goes a long way; therefore, it is necessary to prepare the solder by making sure it is cut and ready to use. These instructions explain how to create "pallions" or chips of solder which are then later placed on metal joints before heating with a torch.

YOU WILL NEED

- solder sheet or solder wire
- shop shears
- small container with lid

1 For sheet solder, use shop shears and make a number of parallel cuts into a corner of the sheet.

2 Cut across each parallel cut with shop shears in order to make tiny squares of solder. (A small glass jar works well for storing solder.)

3 For wire solder, follow step 2 above.

Tip

Mark solder clearly so as not to get the different types mixed up. Mark with a pen or scratch letters H, M, E on solder sheets to help identify them. Mark the outside of the storage container as well.

PREPARING TO SOLDER AND USING FLUX

Once the metal piece has been cleaned in a pickle and the solder is cut and ready to use, it is time to prepare for soldering. This includes using some flux in order to aid in dissolving oxides. Flux also helps to keep solder in place before heating it.

1 Make sure the joint to be soldered is filed flat so that both sides fit flush against each other.

2 Set the metal piece to be soldered on a soldering pad. (If necessary, secure with straight pins, small nails, and/or binding wire.)

3 With a brush, apply a coating of flux over the surface of the metal piece(s) to be soldered (A). A lot of flux isn't necessary; however, the heat from the torch will burn off any excess, and there should be enough flux to cover the solder (B).

4 Use a pair of tweezers to pick up a chip of solder (A), and place the solder chip on top of the joint to be connected (B).

YOU WILL NEED

- metal piece(s) to be soldered
- flux
- small brush
- soldering pad
- hard solder
- tweezers

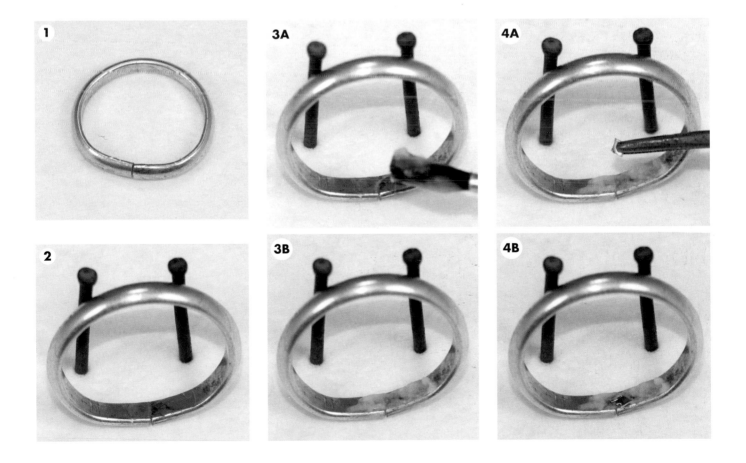

HEATING SOLDER

This next technique assumes the metal piece(s) are prepared for soldering, which means they have been pickled in a pickling solution, placed on a soldering pad, coated with flux, and chips of solder have been appropriately applied. Again, remember to conform to the necessary safety precautions described earlier in this section before using a torch.

1 Turn on the torch following the manufacturer's directions. Most small butane torches have a switch for releasing the gas and then one for igniting it, so a torch striker may not be necessary. For propane-based torches and acetylene, you will probably have to turn a knob to release the gas a little, and then use the striker to start the flame.

2 Once the flame is lit, adjust the release of the gas until the flame is pointed.

3 Resist the urge to point the flame directly at the solder. First, warm up the area around it and allow the flux to slowly evaporate; otherwise, the solder will more than likely pop or fly off the joint it was placed on earlier.

4 Move the flame around the piece to create an even distribution of heat.

5 The flux should dry and turn white as it evaporates. If it bubbles or boils, the flame is being applied too rapidly to the metal piece. Pull the flame away to stop the bubbling then reapply the heat slowly.

6 When the metal around the joints that have solder placed on them turn a dull or cherry red, the piece is hot enough to move the flame closer to the solder.

7 Always keep the flame moving even if only slightly. Heat the solder until it flows into the joint, and then remove the flame, and turn off the torch.

8 Use tweezers to place the hot metal into a jar of water to quench it; then put it in the pickle pot to clean it. When you remove the metal from the pickle, it will have a frosted finish

9 If more soldering is necessary, repeat the Preparing to Solder and Using Flux method on page 119, but this time use medium or easy solder before moving on to the Heating Solder method.

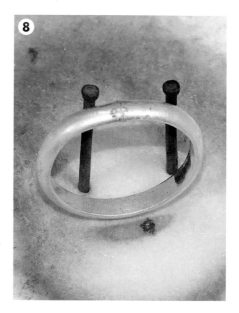

SWEAT SOLDERING

Layering one piece of metal on top of another piece of metal is called sweat soldering. Two piece of metal are being connected, but there are no joints involved necessarily.

YOU WILL NEED

- metal piece(s) prepared to solder
- soldering pad
- soldering tripod and screen
- tweezers
- jar of water
- torch
- torch striker

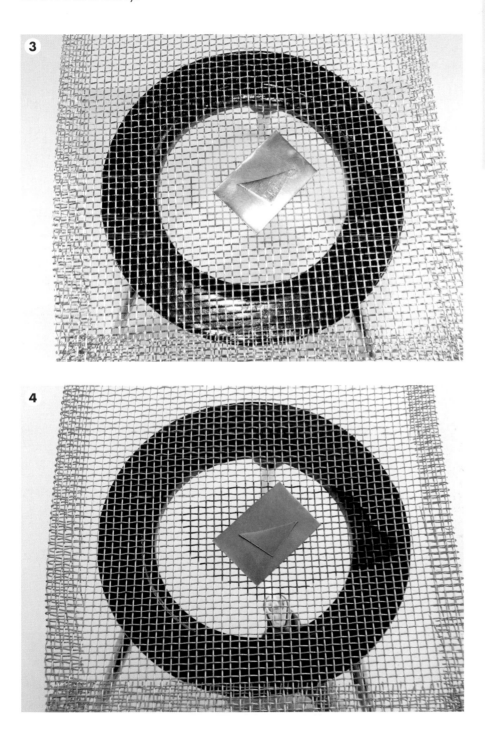

1 Follow the same procedures described in Preparing to Solder and Using Flux, but instead of placing the flux and solder on a joint, place them on top of a piece of metal that will have another piece connected on top of it.

2 Ensure that the top piece of metal has also been pickled, and place it over the fluxed area and solder chips. Depending on the size of the top piece, more than one solder chip may be necessary.

3 Place these stacked pieces on top of a screen and place the screen on top of a tripod.

4 Turn on the torch and hold it under the screen. Because one piece of metal is on top of the solder, it isn't possible to see the solder "flow"; however, when the solder does flow, the top piece will settle flat against the bottom piece. Once this occurs, the soldering is complete.

5 Use tweezers to place the hot metal into a jar of water to quench it.

Projects

Once you have read through the techniques and gathered the necessary supplies, try one of these easy soldering projects. Be sure to follow all the safety precautions. The more experience you have handling the torch and other tools, the more comfortable you will become with making soldered jewelry.

TRIPLE-WRAP STERLING RING

A triple-wrapped effect is created in this chunky ring that incorporates three rings soldered together. Two are soldered up against each other while a thinner ring of silver accents the center. The finished ring constructed in this project is a size 11. To make it smaller or larger, simply adjust the length of the half-round and round wire used to form the rings.

1   Use a large file to file the ends of both pieces of half-round wire to ensure the ends are evenly flat.

2   Take both half-round pieces of wire, wrap them around the ring mandrel approximately at the size 11 mark, and use a rawhide hammer to form them around the mandrel.

(continued)

2

YOU WILL NEED

- hard silver solder
- easy silver solder
- soldering pad
- tweezers
- jar of water
- torch
- torch striker
- pickle
- binding wire
- ring mandrel
- rawhide hammer
- large file
- 320 extra-fine sandpaper
- third hand tool
- two pairs of chain-nose pliers
- two 3" (8 cm) pieces of 8-gauge (3.2 mm) half-round sterling wire
- 3" (8 cm) 16-gauge (1.3 mm) round sterling wire

3 Pull the rings off the mandrel, and use chain-nose pliers to align the ends of the wire. Do not worry about the rings being perfectly round at this point. Pickle the rings.

4 Secure one of the rings in a third hand, and use hard solder to join the ends together (page 120). (If a third hand is not available, lean the ring against an additional soldering pad or use straight pins to prop the ring up during the soldering process.)

5 Repeat step 4 for the second ring so that both have their joints soldered closed.

6 Put the rings back on the mandrel, and gently shape them using a rawhide hammer.

7 Pull the rings off the mandrel, and sand one side of each of the rings against a piece of sandpaper placed on a flat surface. The two sanded surfaces will be joined; sanding helps to ensure full contact when the two rings are soldered together.

8 Pickle both rings to clean them before continuing.

9 Use binding wire to secure the two rings together, and hold them using a third hand or lean them up against an additional soldering pad.

10 Use hard solder to solder the edges together. Because it is not possible to solder all around the rings at the same time, you will need to solder about a third of the area around the ring at a time.

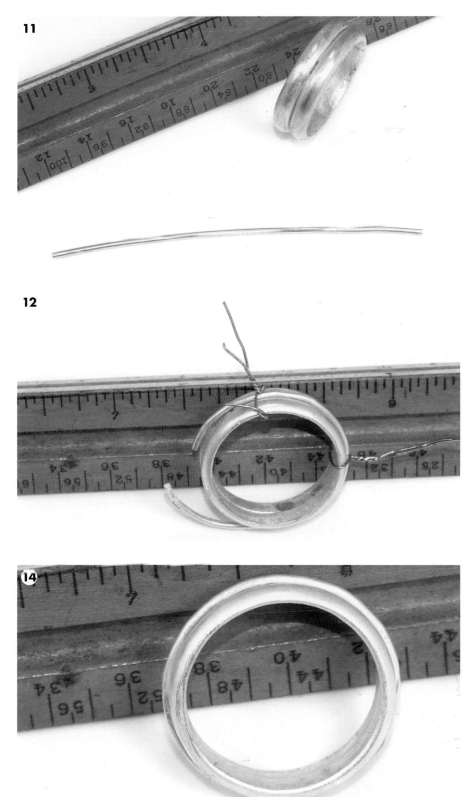

11 File the ends of the 16-gauge wire piece, and pickle the wire as well as the rings previously soldered together.

12 Use binding wire to secure the round wire in the groove between the soldered-together rings.

13 Similarly to step 10, solder the round wire into the groove between the rings, working about a third of the area around the ring at a time but using easy solder this time.

14 After pickling the ring, it is ready for polishing. (See Chain Making, page 73, for polishing techniques).

Tip

Whenever troubleshooting any soldering problems, check cleanliness first. Pickle, metal, and solder all must be clean of contaminants. When in doubt, clean it!

YOU WILL NEED

- hard silver solder
- soldering pad
- tweezers
- jar of water
- torch
- torch striker
- pickle
- oval bracelet mandrel
- rawhide hammer

- needle files
- ruler
- two 6" (15 cm) pieces of 12-gauge (2 × 2 mm) square sterling wire
- ten 8-mm pieces of 12-gauge (2 × 2 mm) square sterling wire

WRIGHT ALIGNMENT BANGLE

The architectural look of this sterling bangle bracelet is reminiscent of the straight lines that were a trademark style of architect Frank Lloyd Wright. Pieces of square wire make up an outside frame, and then smaller pieces of square wire are spaced at intervals inside of this frame.

1 File the ends of all the wire pieces to ensure they are flat. The ends of all the shorter wire pieces should fit flush against the sides of the longer wire pieces.

(continued)

1

2

5

2 Take two of the smaller wire pieces, and solder them inside both ends of the two longer wire pieces so that a rectangular frame is formed.

3 Measure ½" (3.8 cm) from one end of the frame, solder another smaller wire piece inside the frame. Repeat this so that there are two more wire pieces soldered on one end of the frame.

4 Repeat step 3 for the opposite end of the frame.

5 Locate the center of the frame, and solder four more short wire pieces in the center that are also ½" (3.8 cm) apart.

6

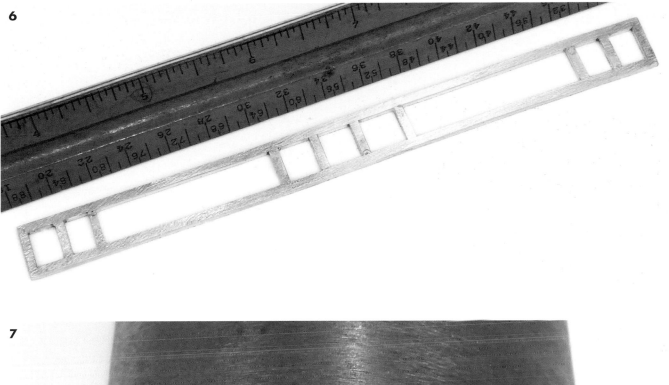

7

6 Use a needle file to file all areas where the wire ends join inside of the frame.

7 With a rawhide hammer and bracelet mandrel, shape the bracelet around the mandrel.

8 The bracelet is now ready for polishing. (See the Chain Making, page 73, for polishing techniques).

Tip

Joints must fit well before the soldering process can even begin. Solder should not be used to fill gaps left by poor fitting. Spend time filing pieces to ensure areas where joints will be soldered fit precisely.

JASPER CABOCHON
PRONGED SETTING PENDANT

Fabrication and soldering skills are both important in this cabochon pendant project. Square wire sections are hand-filed to create half-lap joints which are soldered together and then wrapped around a large jasper cabochon.

1. With medium solder, connect the 2-mm jump ring to the end of the 1¼" (3 cm) piece of wire. This piece will be the "spine" of the cabochon when the setting is complete.

(continued)

YOU WILL NEED

- one 30 × 40-mm jasper cabochon pendant
- medium silver solder
- easy silver solder
- soldering pad
- tweezers
- wire cutters
- jar of water
- torch
- torch striker
- pickle
- large file
- ruler
- one 1¼" (3 cm) piece of 16-gauge square (1.3 × 1.3-mm) sterling wire
- three 2" (5 cm) pieces of 16-gauge square (1.3 × 1.3-mm) sterling wire
- one 4-mm 18-gauge twisted (1 mm) sterling jump ring
- one 2-mm 18-gauge (1 mm) sterling jump ring

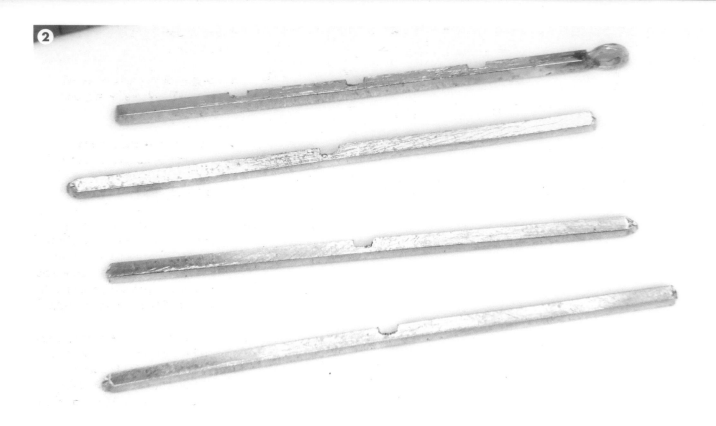

2 In the center of each of the three longer pieces of wire, the "ribs" of the piece, file square recesses halfway through. Do the same to the spine at equally spaced thirds. This will allow the ribs to join the spine in half-lap joints. It is important that these joints fit perfectly flush and tight.

3 After filing the recesses, pickle, and then fit the longer rib wire pieces into the shorter spine piece. This is called a half-lap joint.

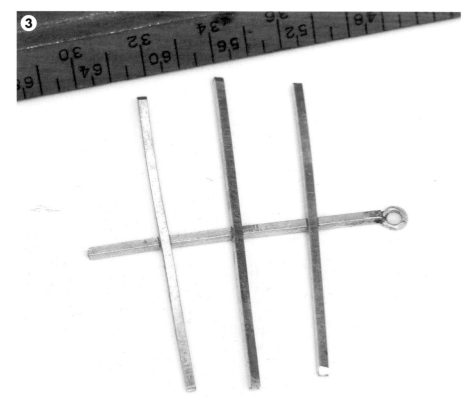

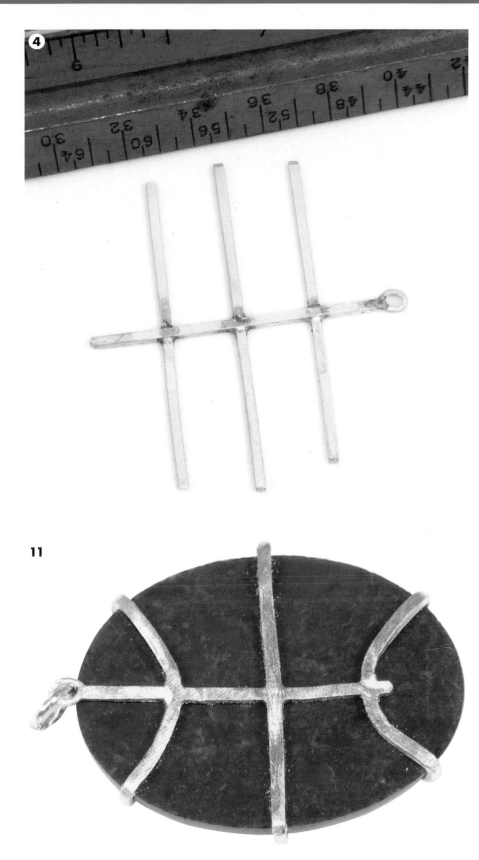

4 Solder each half-lap joint using easy solder.

5 File any rough areas, especially around the soldered joints, and clean the piece.

6 Center the cabochon on the spine, and wrap each end of the middle wire ribs up and around the cabochon.

7 Bend the outside rib sections at approximately 45-degree angles and wrap the ends up and around the cabochon. At this point, there will be six square-shaped prongs around the cabochon fitting somewhat snugly.

8 Using wire cutters, create the prongs by cutting each of the six wires so that they only extend about ³⁄₁₆" (4.8 mm) above the edge of the cabochon. Do not cut them too short.

9 Use a file to taper each square prong.

10 Place the file against each prong and push the finished prongs tightly against the cabochon.

11 Attach the 4 mm twisted wire jump ring to the soldered 2 mm jump ring.

(See page 73, for polishing techniques).

Tip

Remember this series of steps when soldering: heat the soldering pad; then heat the metal; and finally heat the solder. When the solder balls up, keep the flame always moving gently and pointed toward the solder a few more minutes until the solder flows.

TWO-TONE TEARDROP EARRINGS

In this project, fabrication techniques, such as Sawing, Piercing, and Filing, are combined with the Sweat Soldering technique. The result is a two-tone metal design that is simple to make but quite elegant. Refer to Metal Fabrication, page 88, for more information on the techniques used in this project.

YOU WILL NEED

- easy silver solder
- soldering screen and tripod
- tweezers
- jar of water
- torch
- torch striker
- pickle

- needle files
- jeweler's saw, blade, and beeswax
- drill press and drill bit
- two 30 × 15-mm paper teardrop templates
- two 15 × 10-mm paper teardrop templates

- glue
- 22-gauge (0.7 mm) sterling silver sheet
- 24-gauge (0.5 mm) copper sheet
- sterling silver ear hooks
- chain-nose pliers

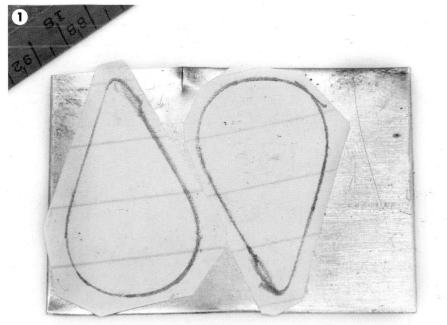

1 Glue the larger teardrop paper templates onto sterling sheet, and cut them out with a jeweler's saw.

(continued)

2 Glue the smaller teardrop paper templates onto copper sheet (A), and cut them out with a jeweler's saw (B).

3 File all around the sides of each of the four teardrop shapes. Be sure that the two pieces of each size are identical.

4 Pickle all four teardrop pieces, and then set the silver teardrop pieces on top of a soldering screen and tripod.

5 Place a small amount of easy solder on top of the piece, and place one of the copper teardrop pieces on top of the solder.

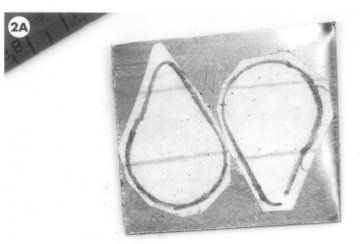

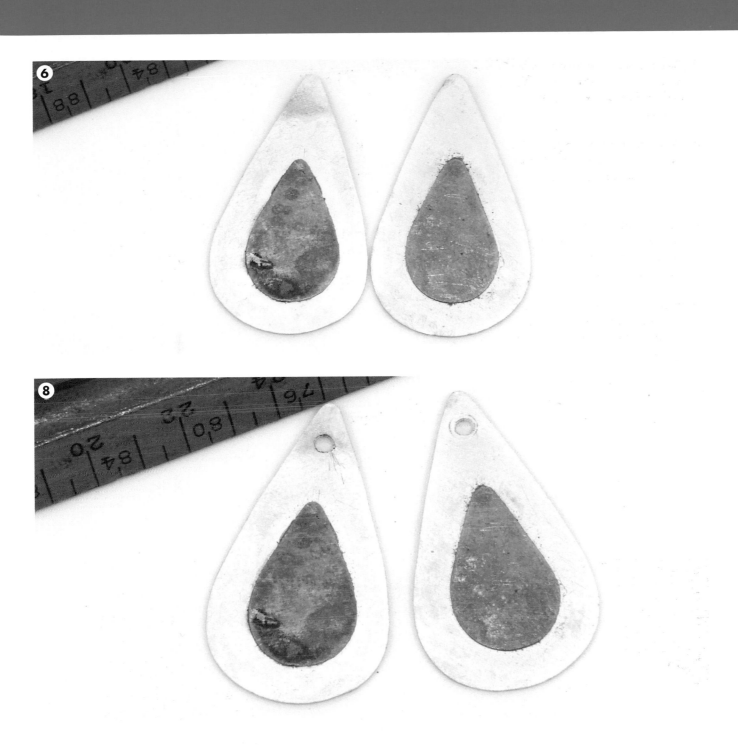

6 Following the Sweat Soldering technique (page 121), use a torch to heat under the screen and solder the copper piece to the silver piece.

7 Repeat steps 5 and 6 for the other earring.

8 Use a drill press to drill a hole at the top of each teardrop piece.

9 Clean and polish each teardrop piece. (See Chain Making, page 73, for polishing techniques.)

10 Use chain-nose pliers to open the loop on each ear hook, slip this loop through the hole on the top of each teardrop, and close the loop back up.

METAL CLAY

Only around since the 1990s, metal clay is relatively new to the jewelry-making world. In this brief amount of time, it has become extremely popular with all kinds of jewelry artists, from those who originally worked with metal to bead lovers as well. This clay is a combination of water, metal particles (silver, copper, brass, or gold), and natural binding materials. Similar to polymer clay, it is possible to cut, roll, and form this material into all kinds of shapes and textures. However, unlike other clays, metal clay must be fired at higher temperatures in order to burn out the organic materials. Once these are gone, the clay becomes a solid piece of metal. It is as amazing as it sounds, and while those who have been working with this material seriously for years have created extremely intricate jewelry designs and developed a huge number of metal clay techniques, the basics are quite achievable for anyone who is ready to experiment and practice with this remarkable medium.

Tools and Supplies

Because this medium starts out as clay and ends up as hard metal, almost any tool used for clay or metal (like those discussed in Metal Fabrication, page 85, and Polymer Clay, page 177) can be used with metal clay. Hand tools and other basics (see General Jewelry-Making Tools, page 9) are also necessary, depending on the final jewelry piece. Then there is the large selection of tools designed primarily for metal clay as well as the clay itself to consider when deciding to make metal clay jewelry. As far as tools, only a small number are needed for the basics such as rolling, forming, and firing. There are many different clays available in all kinds of metals and with various firing requirements.

Metal Clay Brands: The clay is made by two manufacturers, both based in Japan. Aida Chemical Industries makes Art Clay, and Mitsubishi Materials makes Precious Metal Clay (PMC). Art Clay lovers will swear that product is best, and PMC users are loyal to their chosen brand as well.

Types of Metal: The metal clay jewelry maker has just about as much choice in metal as the traditional metalsmith. This includes fine silver, copper, brass, and gold, all of which are available as metal clay.

Standard-Fire Clay: Most metal clays that are considered standard or the traditional form require firing in a kiln. That is, the clay needs very high temperatures to fire, as high as 1650°F (900°C) in some cases, in order for the organic material to burn out. The advantage to using this clay is that larger pieces can be made with it.

Low-Fire Clay: For small jewelry components, low fire clay is a good way to go because it can be fired using a butane torch or hot pot, both of which fire at lower temperature than a kiln. For those just starting with metal clay or the hobbyist who doesn't want to invest in an expensive kiln, this is a good option.

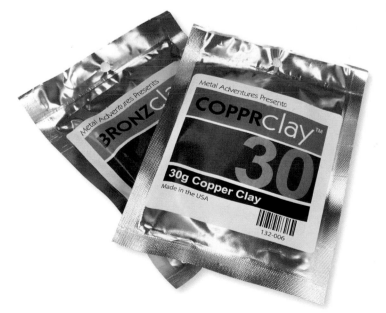

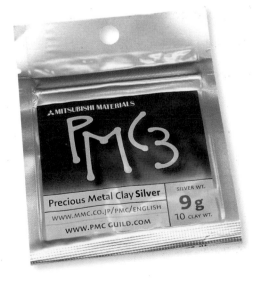

Metal Clay Paper or Sheet: Though it is possible to roll out clay and create a thin sheet, it is handy to buy it already made because it is very, very thin. It is so thin that it is possible to fold it like a piece of paper.

Metal Clay Paste or Slip: Clay paste is used to help stick items together, sort of like glue. While it is possible to buy premade paste or slip, it is pretty easy to make it by mixing a little water with unfired pieces of clay scraps and keeping it stored in a small jar.

Metal Clay Syringe: Paste also comes packaged in a syringe. This allows a little more control over the paste, which makes it possible to create decorative elements like lines across a metal piece.

Roller: A small plastic tube is used for rolling out the clay. These are available from most suppliers who sell metal clay and are very inexpensive; however, it is also possible to use a piece of PVC pipe as a substitute. Some of the fancier rollers have additional rings that connect on both ends of the roller to help calibrate the thickness of the clay while rolling.

Craft Knife: A sharp craft knife with blades that can be replaced is necessary to cut the clay. In general, cutting is done after the clay is rolled out.

Carving Tools: These look similar to dental instruments and are used to carve either wet or dry clay. They are very durable and made out of stainless steel.

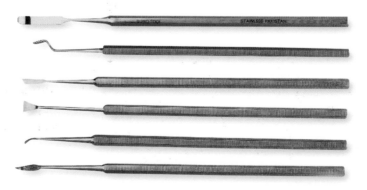

Texture Plates: Metal clay is easily textured, and there are all kinds of texture plates available. Some are made of metal and others are plastic.

Wipe Out or Shaping Tools: Wipe out or shaping tools are good for when a light touch is needed to either remove a mark on wet clay or to gently form the clay. The silicone or rubber tips are angled and soft.

Rubber Stamps (not shown): Typically used for paper crafting, rubber stamps can be used to make impressions into wet clay.

Cutter Sets: Like cookie cutters, use clay cutters to form shapes like stars and hearts very quickly into the clay.

Burnish Brush: After the metal is fired, a stiff burnishing brush helps to remove some of the fire scale left on the metal piece.

Deck of Cards: Use playing cards stacked in equal numbers on either side of the clay to help ensure an even thickness when rolling it out.

Small Straws: Collect drinking straws in different diameters. They work really well for punching small holes through clay.

Small Jars: Good for storing metal clay paste, scraps of clay, and other odds and ends, small jars about the size of a baby food jar are very useful.

Paintbrush: Use small brushes to dab on water or paste while working with the clay.

Nonstick Work Surface: Metal clay is sticky, so that means the work surface must be made of nonstick materials. Vendors sell a number of nonstick products to work on as well as to dry the clay on. Another alternative is to use a clear plastic paper protector, the kind sold at office supply stores.

Graph Paper: Slip a piece of graph paper into a clear paper protector to assist with cutting clay. The lines on the graph paper provide guides to follow.

Metal Clay File or Fine Sandpaper: After a piece of clay has dried, some clean up may be needed around the edges before firing. Fine sandpaper or a file created for metal clay, such as the PMC Greenware Files, can smooth out rough spots on unfired clay.

Spray Bottle: Sometimes the clay can start drying out while working with it, so a little bottle filled with distilled water is useful for rehydrating it.

Distilled Water: Distilled water is cleaner than regular tap water, so it is best to use with clay.

Olive Oil: Clay can be sticky to work with, but a tiny amount of olive oil rubbed on tools and fingers can help keep the stickiness to a minimum.

Liver of Sulfur: To create a patina on fired metal clay pieces, liver of sulfur is an excellent product to use. Many jewelry supply and some art supply companies carry this product. It comes in liquid as well as solid form. The solid form looks like small rocks and must be dissolved in warm water, but it tends to last longer than the liquid form.

Baking Soda: Baking soda is useful for cleaning metal items with water and a burnish brush. It is also good for stopping the patina process when using liver of sulfur.

Kiln: Some metal clay types require high firing temperatures that can only be obtained using a kiln. While there are lots of kilns available, it is a good idea to get one with a pyrometer, which provides an accurate gauge of the temperature. This helps ensure the clay has fired at the right temperature. Programmable kilns are also a very good choice for metal clay work because they come already set with preprogrammed firing cycles designed to fire various types of metal clay, and it is also possible to create specific programs for these kilns as well. Again, this helps make sure the clay fires at the right temperature for the right amount of time. Otherwise, the organic material may not burn out all the way, and the clay will not be completely fired.

Kiln Shelf: This is a tray that slides into the bottom of the kiln. It holds clay pieces as they fire and makes it easier to slide them in and out before and after firing.

Kiln Furniture: Small square pieces of cordierite, these are used to prop up items in a kiln or stack kiln shelves to allow for air to circulate inside of the kiln.

Hot Pot (left): This looks similar to a potpourri pot and can only be used to fire small metal clay items formed with low-fire clay. Though the size and amount of items fired is limited, it is a good choice for beginners or those who just want to dabble with metal clay and are not ready to purchase a kiln.

Torch: A hand-held butane torch has the same function as the hot pot. It is also only useful for low-fire clay items.

Firing Pan: Some forms of clay (such as copper clay) need to be fired along with other materials such as activated carbon granules, so a stainless steel pan with a lid (right) is necessary to house both the clay and the other materials.

Activated Carbon Granules: Brass and copper metal clay must be embedded in activated carbon. This material is available from most vendors who sell copper or brass clay and related metal clay supplies.

Kiln Fork: This is a giant-sized fork used to pick up and remove a firing pan from inside a hot kiln.

Polishing Paper: Polish fired metal clay with micron-graded abrasive paper. It comes in a range of grits from 400 to 8000 and can be used dry or wet.

Letter Stamps: The same metal letter stamps used for metal fabrication can also used for metal clay; however, there are some tools designed for stamping letters into clay as well.

Techniques

Though it is possible to use metalsmithing techniques on metal clay jewelry items that have been fired, this material is very pliable before firing, and has lots of advantages over traditional metal work. It is very easy to form, cut, and texture, so a lot of intricate detail is possible. There is no real limit to what can be done with metal clay, and jewelry artists continue to explore and expand on current methods. However, the basics are relatively easy for anyone new to this medium to learn.

ROLLING CLAY

Usually the first step in working with metal clay is to roll it out on a work surface. Because the clay dries fairly quickly once exposed to air, it is important to have an idea of the intended jewelry design before opening a package of clay.

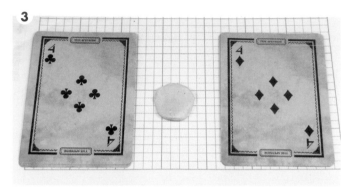

YOU WILL NEED

- metal clay of your choice
- nonstick work surface
- olive oil
- clay roller
- playing cards

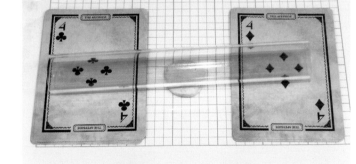

1 Take a few drops of oil and rub it on the clay roller as well as your fingers.

2 Set the clay piece on the nonstick surface.

3 Select six to eight playing cards, separate them into two even stacks, and place them on either side of the clay piece.

4 Press the roller down on the clay (A), and roll it back and forth until it is the thickness desired (B).

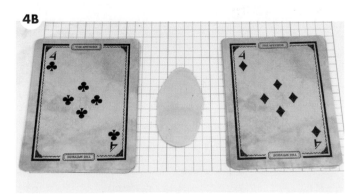

Tip

Placing stacks of playing cards on either side of the clay ensures an even thickness to the clay when rolling it out.

CUTTING CLAY SHAPES

Metal cutters, which look like small cookie cutters, work well to cut out shapes of clay and turn them into charms or other ornaments.

YOU WILL NEED

- choice of metal clay
- nonstick work surface
- olive oil
- clay roller
- playing cards
- craft knife

2

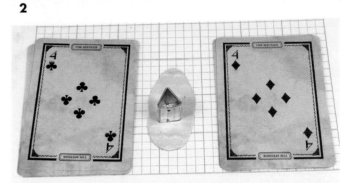

1 Roll out the clay to the desired thickness.

2 Press the cutter into the clay.

3 Pull the cutter up from the clay (A), and remove the clay from inside of it (B).

3A

3B

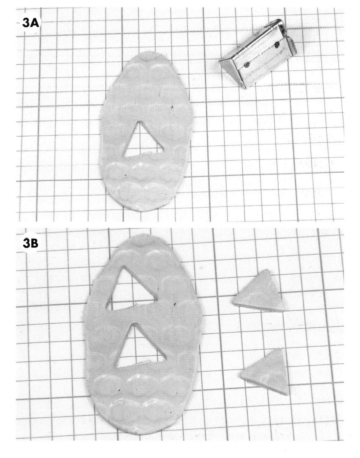

Tip

Clay does not usually stick to metal cutters; however, if stickiness is a concern, rub the edges with a tiny amount of oil. Just remember less is best.

CUTTING AROUND TEMPLATES

Other shapes can be made by using templates. Use purchased templates or create them simply by cutting shapes out of paper or plastic.

YOU WILL NEED

- metal clay of your choice
- clay roller
- nonstick work surface
- playing cards
- olive oil
- craft knife

1 Roll the clay out, and place the template on top of it.

2 Cut around template with a craft knife.

3 Remove the template, and use the craft knife to pull up the edge of the clay to remove it from the rolled piece.

MAKING SLIP

Slip or metal clay paste is useful for sticking items together, much like glue. It is also possible to coat organic materials such as leaves and sticks with paste, and during the firing process, the organic material burns away, leaving a replicated metal piece. This paste is available for purchase, but it is also very easy to make.

YOU WILL NEED

- choice of metal clay
- distilled water
- small paintbrush
- small glass or plastic container

1 In a small container such as a jar or plastic film container, add scraps of metal clay.

2 Pour a small amount of distilled water into the container.

3 Use a paintbrush to stir until the clay has been dissolved by the water.

4 Continue to add clay and water until a spreadable, paste-like consistency is achieved.

Tip

Keep a scrap jar for each type of clay used. These little bits are perfect for turning into slip. Depending on the intended use, it is also helpful to have an assortment of slip, from thin to thick.

LAYERING CLAY PIECES

Also sometimes referred to as appliqué, taking one piece of clay and placing it onto another piece of clay is a useful technique, especially if more than one type of metal is used. It is possible to layer wet or dry clay pieces.

YOU WILL NEED

- metal clay of your choice
- nonstick work surface
- olive oil
- spray bottle or shallow dish of distilled water
- clay roller
- playing cards
- craft knife or cutter
- small paintbrush
- slip

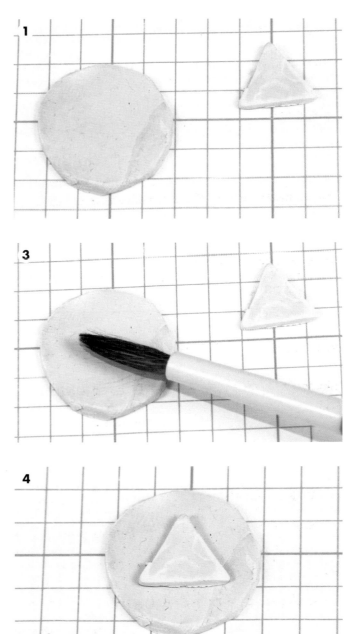

1 Roll the clay out, and use a craft knife or cutter to form desired shapes. At least two are needed

2 Determine which shape will be on the bottom and the top.

3 Use a paintbrush to place a small amount of water on the bottom clay shape.

4 Place the top clay piece on top of the one brushed with water in the previous step.

5 If either of the two pieces is dry or almost dry, use slip instead of just the water as described in step 3.

6 Allow the clay to dry completely before firing.

TEXTURING BEFORE FIRING

Wonderful textures are easy to create in metal clay and they look amazing after firing. Texture plates are perfect for this, but it is also possible to use unusual items such as lace or items found around the house to texture clay.

1 Roll out the clay to the desired thickness.

2 Dab a tiny amount of oil onto the texture plate.

3 Place the plate on top of the clay, and press (A). If the clay is very thick, roll over the plate with the clay roller to make sure the impression is deep enough (B).

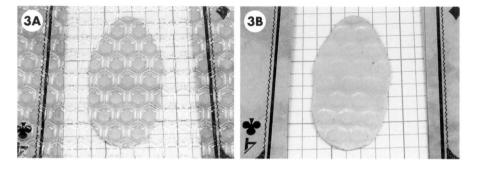

STAMPING CLAY

Rubber stamps or metal stamps are not just for paper and metal. Both can be used to imprint images or text into soft metal clay.

1 Roll out the clay, select a stamp, and add a tiny amount of oil to it.

2 Press the stamp into the clay (A), making sure to press evenly down and pulling up rather than rocking the stamp back and forth (B).

Tip

Start a collection of items to use for texturing such as scraps of lace or other fibers, plastic dinnerware, or just about anything imaginable. Then have fun experimenting with them.

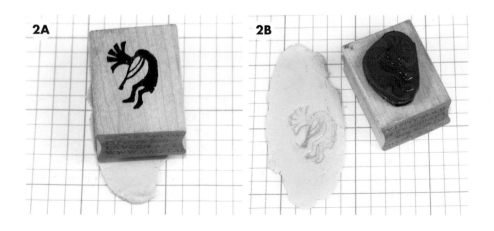

FIRING SILVER METAL CLAY WITH A KILN

The exact temperatures and length of firing vary depending on the type of metal clay, so check the manufacturer's instructions.

YOU WILL NEED

- kiln
- kiln shelf, fiber blanket, or heat-proof container of vermiculite
- heat-resistant gloves
- tweezers
- jar of water

1 After metal clay pieces have dried thoroughly, they are ready to fire. Spread flat items, such as charms or pendants, out on a kiln shelf. It is important that the pieces are not too close together since some air circulation is necessary.

2 Place three-dimensional clay pieces either in a heat-proof container filled with vermiculite or on a fiber blanket.

3 Slide the kiln shelf, blanket, or vermiculite container into the kiln.

4 If the kiln is programmable, follow the instruction manual provided with the kiln to set the correct program. If it is not programmable, set the temperature per the instructions provided with the clay, and time this first cycle. Increase the time again depending on the requirements for the type of clay being fired.

Tip

The kiln will be extremely hot, so use proper safety equipment and common sense. Work in a well-ventilated area and place the kiln on a sturdy heat-resistant surface that has plenty of room around it for air circulation. When the kiln is not in use, it is a good idea to leave it unplugged.

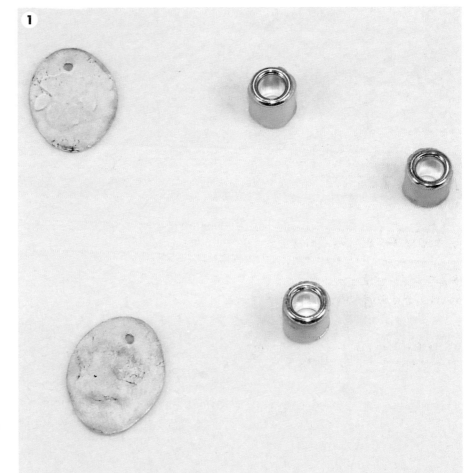

1

5 After the firing cycle is complete, it is fine to turn off the kiln and pull out the fired clay pieces the next day. To pull them out sooner, put on gloves, open the kiln door a little, and close it. This will vent some of the hot air. Venting a few times will help cool down the kiln.

6 With gloves still on, once the kiln is cool enough to open the door completely, pull out the items (shelf, container, or fiber blanket), use tweezers to pick up each clay piece, and place them in water to quench them.

FIRING COPPER OR BRONZE METAL CLAY WITH A KILN

Firing copper or bronze clay in a kiln is very similar to firing silver, but instead of using a kiln shelf, fiber blanket, or container of vermiculite, the dried clay pieces must be placed in a metal firing pan filled with activated carbon granules.

1 Make sure the metal pieces are completely dry before firing them.

2 Fill the pan to a depth of at least 1" (2.5 cm) with the carbon granules.

3 Place the metal clay pieces on top of the carbon granules leaving at least ½" (1.3 cm) between them.

4 Fill the rest of the pan with more carbon granules, and put on the lid.

5 Set four pieces of kiln furniture evenly inside the bottom of the kiln, and place the pan on top of these.

6 Repeat steps 4 through 6 of the instructions for Firing Silver Metal Clay with a Kiln (page 151), using the kiln fork to remove the pan but do not remove the clay pieces from the firing pan until the pan has completely cooled.

YOU WILL NEED

- kiln
- firing pan
- kiln fork
- kiln furniture
- activated carbon granules
- heat-resistant gloves

Tip

Though it may cost a little more, a programmable kiln is a big help when firing metal clay. You still must keep an eye on the kiln for safety reasons, but the programs remove the added burden of having to time each heating cycle. Plus, it could save money in the long run since the firing cycle will be more accurate, and this means a better chance at successful metal clay firings.

FIRING CLAY WITH A TORCH

Only low-fire metal clays can be fired with a hand-held butane torch, and there is an additional restriction of size. These pieces cannot be larger than 20 grams or about the size of a half-dollar coin. However, for those new to clay, this is a good way to learn some of the basics without having to purchase a kiln.

1 Set up the soldering pad, water, and tweezers in a well-ventilated area.

2 Place the metal clay piece on top of the pad.

3 Turn on the torch and start to slowly heat the area around and a few inches (centimeters) away from the clay piece.

YOU WILL NEED

- butane hand-held torch
- soldering pad
- tweezers
- jar of water

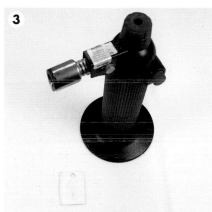

4 Start moving the flame in a circular motion around the clay. This will help it heat evenly. If the clay starts to bubble or look shiny, the flame is too close. Just back up a little.

5 After a few minutes, the piece will begin to smoke because the organic material is being burnt away. Continue to heat the clay piece for a few minutes until it turns bright orange.

6 Continue to heat from two to five minutes. Larger pieces should be heated longer than smaller pieces.

7 Point the torch away from the clay piece, and turn it off.

8 Use tweezers to pick up the fired clay and place it in the jar of water to quench.

FIRING CLAY WITH A HOT POT

An alternative to heating low-fire clay with a torch is a hot pot. Like working with the torch, the hot pot can only accommodate low-fire clay that is under 20 grams, but the advantage is that the hot pot does all of the work.

1 Find a safe location for the pot to fire, like a patio or garage with the door open. Place the pot on a heat-resistant surface, such as tile or cement.

2 Fill the inside pot with fuel, and place it inside of the bottom part of the hot pot.

YOU WILL NEED

- hot pot
- hot pot fuel
- fireplace lighter or match
- tweezers
- heat-resistant gloves
- jar of water

3 Place the thoroughly dried clay items on top of the grate, and place the grate on top of the bottom part of the pot.

4 Insert a fireplace lighter through one of the holes in the bottom of the pot, and ignite the fuel.

5 Place the top part of the hot pot over the grate.

6 The pot takes about 15 minutes to fire completely. Once the firing is done, make sure to wear gloves since the pot is very hot at this point, and take the lid off.

7 Use tweezers to pick up the fired clay pieces and place them in a jar of water.

CLEANING AND POLISHING FIRED METAL CLAY

Once the clay is fired, it becomes solid metal. This means it can be polished and cleaned just like sheet metal or wire (refer to the polishing techniques described in Chain Making, page 73). However, since silver metal clay is fine silver there is no fire-scale to deal with. With a little water and a burnishing brush, it cleans up quickly. Copper and brass fired metal clay can also be cleaned and polished in a similar way; however, to create a higher shine on any fired metal clay, an assortment of wet/dry polishing papers work really well.

1

YOU WILL NEED

- assortment of wet/dry polishing paper

1 Rub the metal piece with wet/dry polishing paper starting with the coarsest grit (400).

2 Continue to work up to finer grits (as high as 8000) to increase the sheen or brightness of the polished metal piece.

3 Stop at any point depending on the finish desired.

Tip

A mirror-finish polish can add a lot to a finished piece of jewelry, but it can also show all kinds of scratches on the metal or other imperfections that might not be noticeable without the high sheen. It might be necessary to use fine sandpaper to remove scratches that show up after polishing. This is just something to keep in mind when deciding how bright the finished jewelry pieces should be polished.

OXIDIZING WITH LIVER OF SULFUR

Lots of detail is possible when it comes to creating with metal clay, and in order to show off details such as stamping and texture, use this simple oxidation process. With liver of sulfur (a stinky but safe product), some warm water, and a little baking soda, areas of the metal clay can be highlighted after firing.

YOU WILL NEED

- liver of sulfur
- baking soda
- two small bowls of water
- tweezers
- paper towels
- microwave
- polishing cloth or 400 grit wet/dry polishing paper

1 Fill two small bowls with water, and microwave one bowl for about 60 seconds. It should be warm, but not boiling.

2 Take a small chunk of liver of sulfur, set it in the warm bowl of water, and use tweezers to stir the water a little. Although it is not harmful, it will start to smell like rotten eggs, so it is a good idea to work in a well-ventilated area.

3 Sprinkle a tablespoon of baking soda in the other bowl of water.

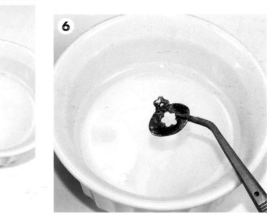

4 Place a metal item in the liver of sulfur water (A), and use tweezers to pull it out after a few seconds (B).

5 Place the metal piece in the bowl with the water and baking soda. (The baking soda neutralizes the effects of the liver of sulfur.)

Tip

Oxidizing is not an exact science. Play around with the amount of liver of sulfur used, the temperature of the water, and the length of time a metal piece is submerged in the liver of sulfur water to see the different finishes that develop on the metal.

6 Pull out the metal item, dry it off with a paper towel, and examine it. If it has the look you want, you are finished. To remove some of the patina, just rub it with a polishing cloth or polishing paper. To make it darker, repeat steps 4 and 5 until it has the desired look.

Projects

Try your hand at making some metal clay jewelry. The projects that follow incorporate the techniques you've just learned. You'll soon discover many new and creative ways to make metal clay jewelry for yourself and your friends.

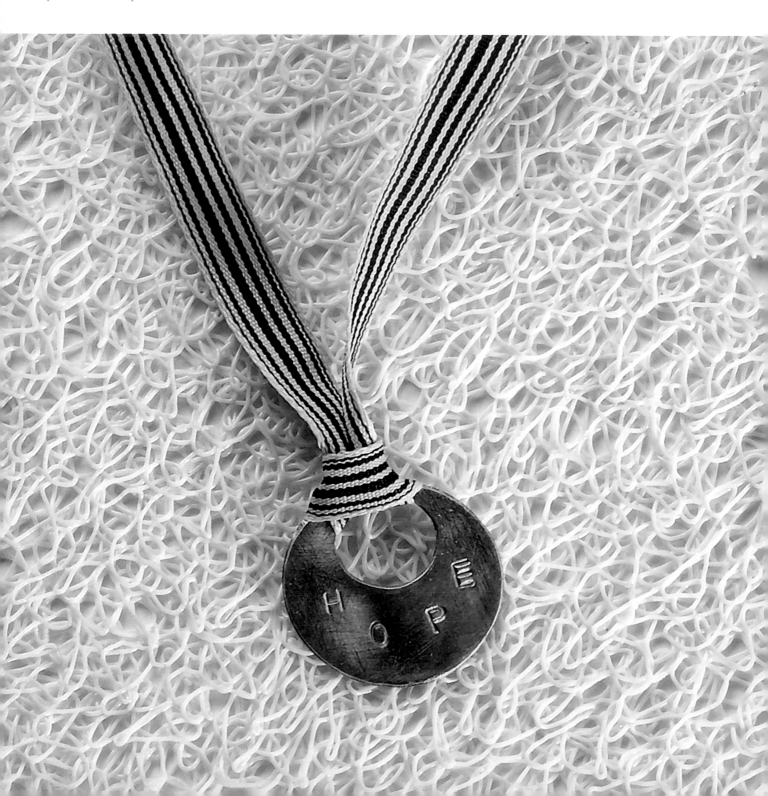

HOPE DONUT PENDANT

Stamping on metal clay is much more forgiving than stamping on sheet metal. Mistakes are not a problem because the clay can simply be rolled up, rolled out, and stamped again. This donut pendant combines rolling, cutting, stamping, and oxidizing techniques.

YOU WILL NEED

- low-fire metal clay
- nonstick work surface
- olive oil
- spray bottle or shallow dish of distilled water
- clay roller
- craft knife
- six playing cards
- fine sandpaper or metal clay file
- burnishing brush or 400-grit wet/dry polishing paper
- one 15-mm diameter cutter
- one 30-mm diameter cutter
- letter stamps (H, O, P, E)
- butane torch, hot pot, or kiln
- liver of sulfur
- baking soda
- two small bowls of water
- tweezers
- paper towels
- microwave
- polishing cloth or 400-grit wet/dry polishing paper
- needle files
- 36" (91.4 cm) of ribbon

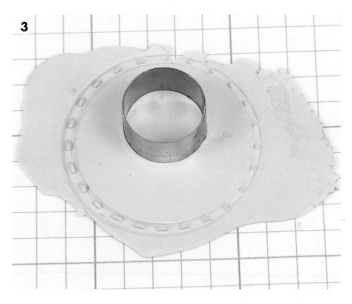

1 Place three playing cards on either side of the clay, and roll out the clay.

2 Use the larger cutter, such as the cap of a vitamin bottle, and cut out a large circle.

3 Position the smaller circle cutter a little above the center of the first circle so that the hole cut is not directly in the center. Remove excess clay inside the smaller cutter and around the large circle.

(continued)

4 Use a craft knife to smooth out the outer edge of the outside circle, if necessary.

5 Beginning just off center to the left and under the second hole cut, press the letter "O" into the clay.

6 To the right of this (again off center but this time to the right), press the letter "P" into the clay.

7 On the left side of the center hole, press the letter "H" into the clay.

8 On the right side of the center hole, press the letter "E" into the clay.

9 Allow the piece to dry thoroughly, and once dry, clean gently around the edges with fine sandpaper or metal clay file.

10 Follow manufacturer's instructions for firing. (Since this is low-fire, a hot pot or butane torch will do.)

11 After the piece is fired and cool enough to handle, clean it by rubbing it under water with a burnishing brush or clean it with 400-grit wet/dry polishing paper.

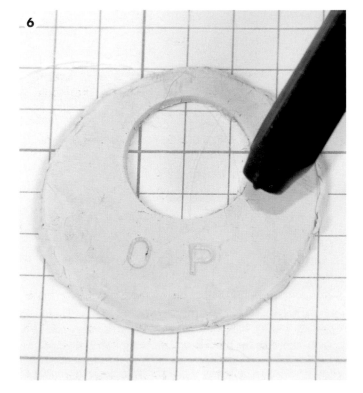

12

13A

14

12 Using the Oxidizing with Liver of Sulfur method, page 155, add a patina to the pendant.

13 Fold the ribbon in half (A), insert the folded part through the hole in the pendant, and insert the end of the ribbons through the fold (B).

14 Pull to secure the ribbon around the hole in the pendant.

15 Tie the ends of the ribbon together using an overhand knot.

Tip

Keep a pad and pencil next to your work area as you work with metal clay and take notes of details such as how thick the piece was rolled, size of cutters used, and so on. This way, it will be easier to duplicate the process and make an identical piece.

13B

ANCIENT KOKOPELLI CHARM

A little oxidation makes this charm look like an ancient artifact. Techniques include rolling, stamping, and oxidizing. This charm could be worn on a chain, but it also looks great with beads, such as the picture agate, silver, and natural onyx beads in the photo, thus combining Bead Stringing and Metal Clay techniques.

1 Put two playing cards on either side of the clay, and roll it out.

2 Place the stamp upside down onto the clay, and use a craft knife to cut around the stamp in order to create a rectangle shape.

(continued)

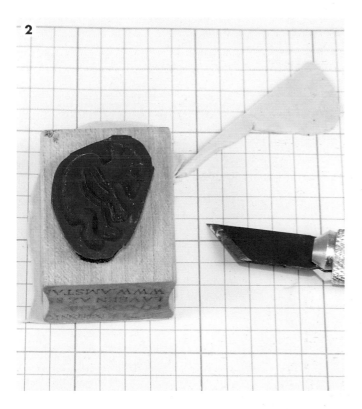

- low-fire metal clay
- Kokopelli stamp
- straw
- 6-mm sterling jump ring
- chain-nose pliers
- crimping pliers
- two 2 × 2-mm sterling crimp beads
- sixty 6-mm picture agate beads
- two 12-mm onyx barrel-shaped beads
- four 6.5-mm sterling daisy spacer beads
- one 11-mm sterling lobster claw clasp and attached ring
- one 4.5-mm soldered closed jump ring
- fine-grit sandpaper
- nonstick work surface
- olive oil
- spray bottle or shallow dish of distilled water
- clay roller
- four playing cards
- fine sandpaper or metal clay file
- burnishing brush
- craft knife
- butane torch, hot pot, or kiln
- liver of sulfur
- baking soda
- two small bowls of water
- tweezers
- paper towels
- microwave
- polishing cloth or 400-grit wet/dry polishing paper
- needle files

3 Cut a hole at the top of the rectangle with a straw.

4 Dab a tiny amount of oil onto the stamp, and press it into the clay.

5 Allow the piece to dry thoroughly, and once dry, clean gently around the edges with fine sandpaper or metal clay file.

6 Follow manufacturer's instructions for firing. (Since this is low-fire clay, a hot pot or butane torch will do.)

7 After the piece is fired and cool enough to handle, clean it by rubbing it under water with a burnishing brush or clean it with 400-grit wet/dry polishing paper. To remove any scratches, use fine sandpaper.

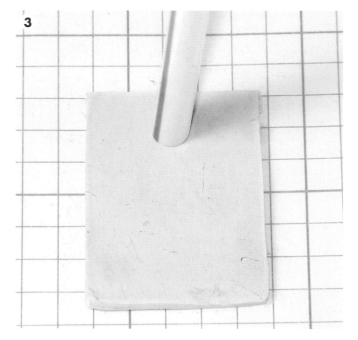

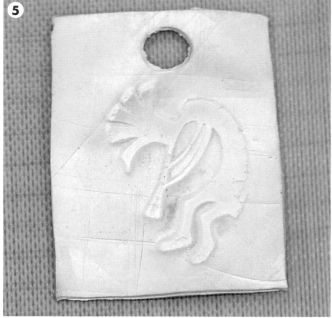

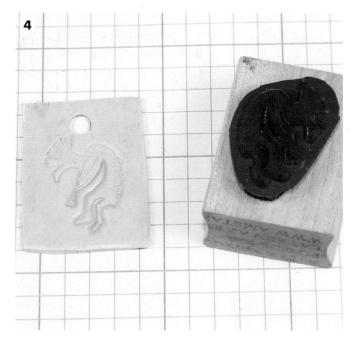

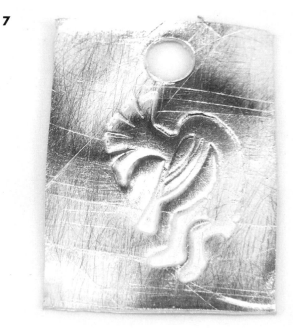

8 Using the Oxidizing with Liver of Sulfur method (page 155), add a patina to the pendant, and then use more wet/dry polishing paper to remove the patina around the outside of the Kokopelli image.

9 Add a jump ring to the top of the charm.

10 Using techniques from the Bead Stringing, page 24, attach a crimp bead and soldered jump ring to one end of the beading wire, and string on beads in this order: twenty-nine agate beads, one silver bead, one onyx bead, one silver bead, and one agate bead.

8

9

11

11 Slip the jump ring of the charm onto the beading wire, and string on more beads in this order: one agate bead, one silver bead, one onyx bead, one silver bead, and twenty-nine agate beads.

12 Finish the other end of the necklace with a lobster clay clasp and another crimp bead, trimming off excess beading wire as necessary.

YOU WILL NEED

- copper metal clay
- four 10 to 12-mm cutters, one each heart, club, spade, diamond
- eight 6-mm copper jump rings
- one 7 × 14-mm copper lobster claw clasp
- 6½" (17.8 cm) of 3-mm copper link chain
- two chain-nose pliers
- nonstick work surface
- olive oil
- spray bottle or shallow dish of distilled water
- clay roller
- six playing cards
- awl
- fine sandpaper or metal clay file
- burnishing brush
- kiln
- firing pan
- kiln fork
- kiln furniture
- activated carbon granules
- heat-resistant gloves
- liver of sulfur
- baking soda
- two small bowls of water
- tweezers
- paper towels
- microwave
- polishing cloth or 400-grit wet/dry polishing paper
- needle files

VEGAS COPPER CHARM BRACELET

This lucky charm bracelet was inspired by card players and one of the luckiest cities in the world, Las Vegas. Heart, spade, diamond, and club shapes were cut from copper clay, fired, and then attached to an antiqued chain. A little oxidation helps the charms match the chain that already came with a patina.

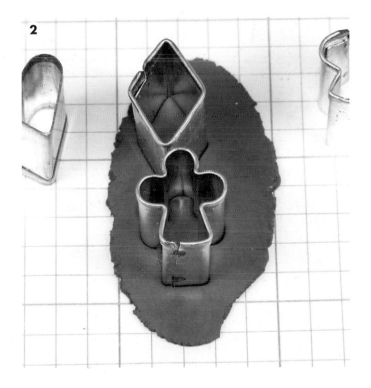

1 Put three playing cards on either side of the clay, and roll it out.

2 Take the cutters and cut out: two hearts, two clubs, two diamonds, and two spades.

(continued)

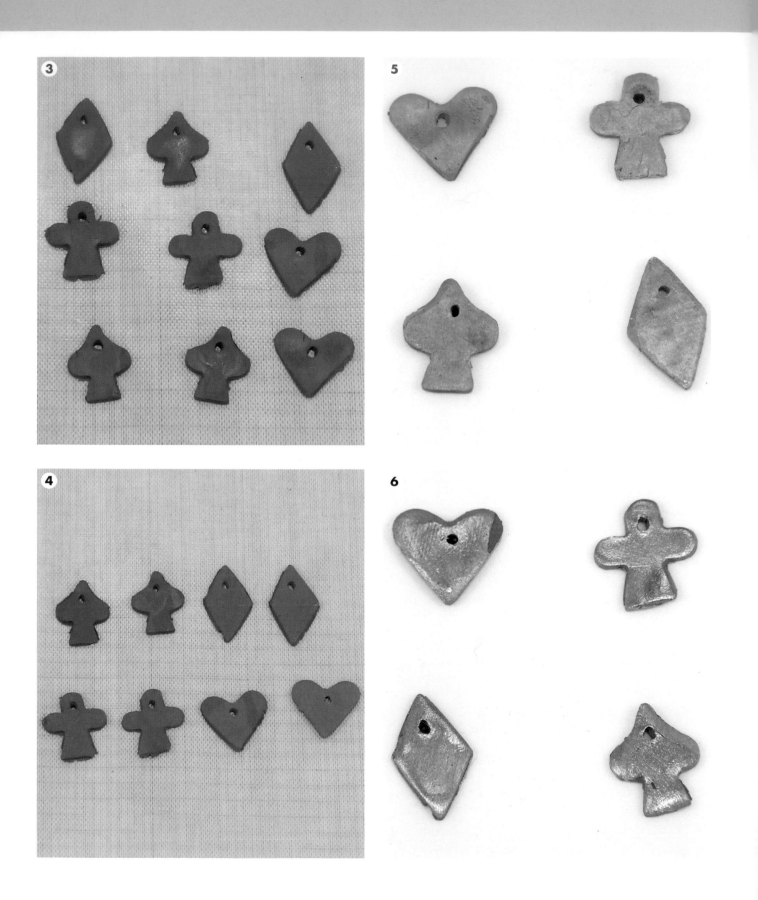

9

3 Use an awl to pierce a hole at the top of each shape while the clay is still wet.

4 Allow the pieces to dry thoroughly, and once dry, clean gently around the edges with fine sandpaper or metal clay file.

5 Follow the technique instructions for Firing Copper or Bronze Metal Clay with a Kiln, page 152.

6 After the pieces are fired and cool enough to handle, clean them by rubbing them under water with a burnishing brush or clean them with 400-grit wet/dry polishing paper. To remove any scratches, use fine sand paper.

7 Using the Oxidizing with Liver of Sulfur (page 155), add a patina to the charms.

8 Add a clasp to one end of the chain and a jump ring to the other end of the chain.

9 Count the links on the chain to determine where to add charms so they are evenly attached to the chain; then add a jump ring to the top of each charm, and connect the jump rings to the selected links.

COPPER CLAY HAMMER-TIME EARRINGS

Though metal clay can be textured before firing, just like regular metal it can be textured after firing as well. This fabrication technique uses a ball-peen hammer to texture stick-shaped copper clay pieces after they have been fired. While only two textured-stick copper pieces are needed to make these earrings, it is a good idea to make more than just two, so you can make multiple pairs of earrings.

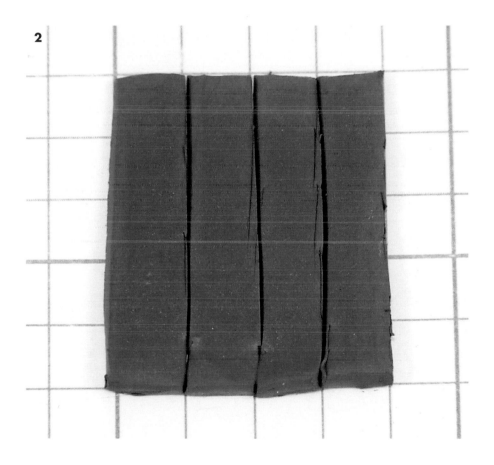

2

YOU WILL NEED

- copper metal clay
- craft knife
- clear nonstick work surface over graph paper
- olive oil
- spray bottle or shallow dish of distilled water
- clay roller
- six playing cards
- awl
- fine sandpaper or metal clay file
- burnishing brush
- kiln
- firing pan
- kiln fork
- kiln furniture
- activated carbon granules
- heat-resistant gloves
- polisher
- anvil
- ball-peen hammer
- copper ear hooks
- 8" (20 cm) 21-gauge (0.7 mm) dead-soft round copper wire
- needle files

1 Put three playing cards on either side of the clay, and roll it out.

2 Each square on the graph paper used for this project should be ¼" (6 mm) in diameter. Using a craft knife and the lines on the graph paper as a guide, cut out some rectangles of clay that are five squares long and one square wide.

(continued)

3 Separate the rectangles (A), and use an awl to pierce a hole at the top of each rectangle while the clay is still wet (B).

4 Allow the pieces to dry thoroughly, and once dry, clean gently around the edges with fine sandpaper or metal clay file.

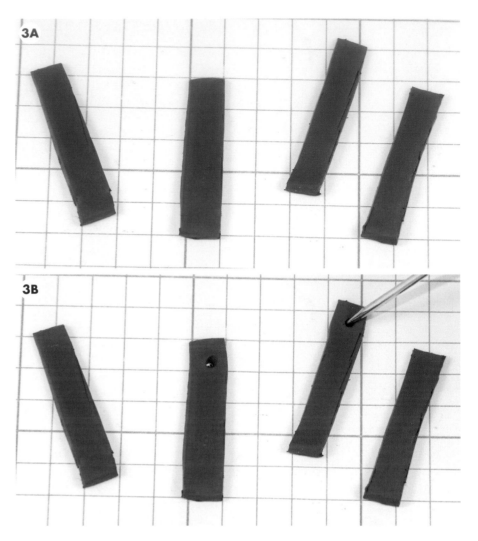

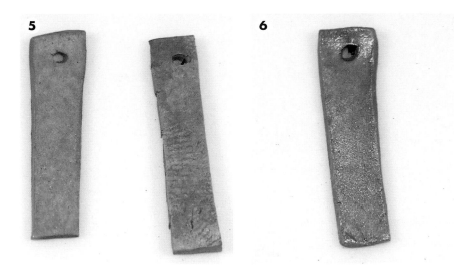

5 Follow the instructions for Firing Copper or Bronze Metal Clay with a Kiln on page 152.

6 After the pieces are fired and cool enough to handle, clean them by rubbing them under water with a burnishing brush or clean them with 400-grit wet/dry polishing paper. To remove any scratches, use fine sandpaper.

7 Polish the rectangles, and then texture them using a ball-peen hammer. (See the Chain Making, page 73, for polishing techniques, and the Texturing Metal technique, page 92.)

8 Using copper wire, make a wrapped loop (see Wire Work, page 47) and slip one of the rectangles onto the loop before closing the wire wraps.

9 Make another loop at the top, and slip on an ear hook.

10 Repeat steps 8 and 9 for the second earring.

Tip

A kiln takes a fair amount of electricity to operate, so it is a good idea to connect it to its own breaker. Always fire more than just a few pieces in order to conserve energy and save on the electric bill.

FROSTED SILVER DISK EARRINGS

Because metal clay becomes solid metal after firing, it is possible to attach solid metal pieces, such as wire or findings, to the clay before firing. Once the pieces are fired, they become fused together. This method for adding a bail to a metal clay piece is used in this earring project. Texturing is also involved, and by polishing only the raised areas of the metal, the finished pieces have an interesting frosted affect.

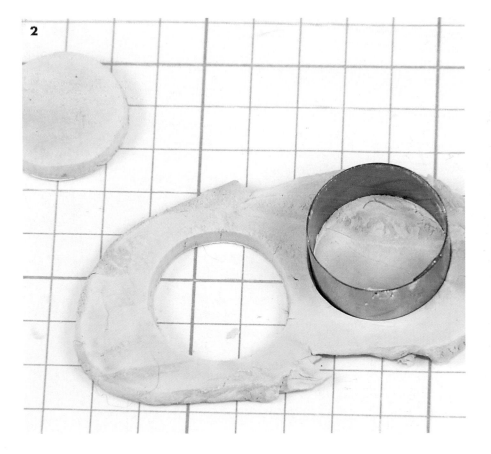

1 Place nine playing cards on either side of the clay, and roll out the clay.

2 Use the circular-shaped cutter, and cut out two round pieces of clay.

(continued)

3 Add a dab of olive oil onto the texture plate, place it on top of the two round clay pieces, and press down.

4 Pick up the plate, turn it a half turn, place it back on top of the clay pieces, and again, press down.

5 Insert a piece of fine silver wire into the side of each of the round clay pieces, and allow them to dry.

6 Once the clay is dry, clean gently around the edges with fine sandpaper or metal clay file.

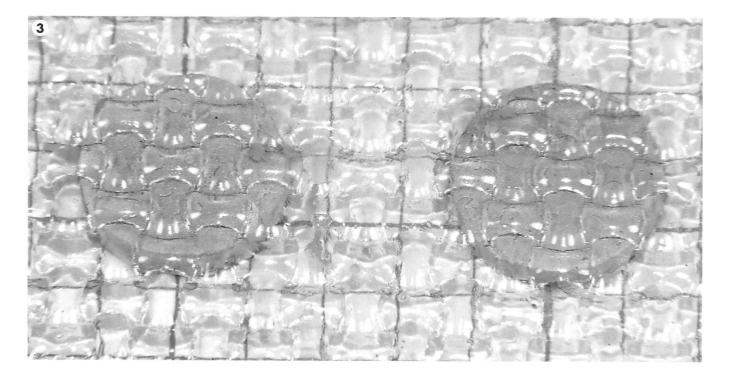

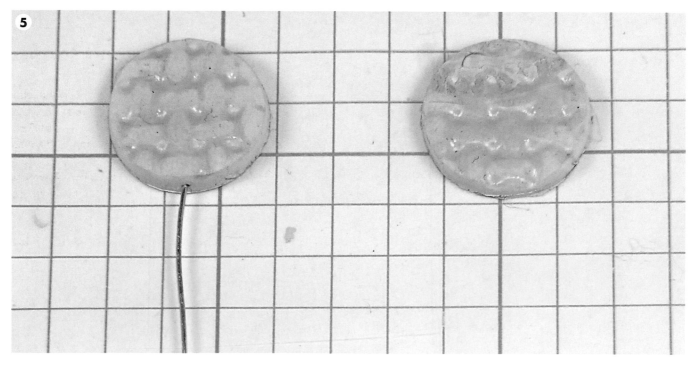

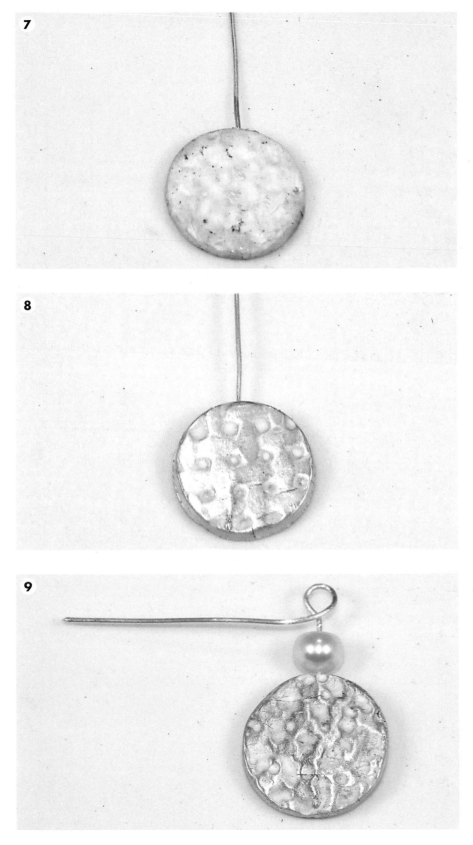

7 Follow manufacturer's instructions for firing. (Since this is low-fire clay, a hot pot or butane torch will do.)

8 After the piece is fired and cool enough to handle, rub it with 400-grit wet/dry polishing paper, then 600-grit paper, followed by 1200-grit paper. Don't worry about getting into the nooks and crannies of the clay. Leave these areas a frosted color and instead polish the higher textured areas of each round piece. Be extra careful not to damage the wire that is now connected to the fired clay piece.

9 Slip a pearl bead onto the wire, and use chain-nose and round-nose pliers to make a wrapped loop at the top. Use wire cutters to trim off excess wire. (See the Wire Work section, page 47, for this technique.) Repeat this for the other round piece.

10 Attach an ear hook to the top of each round piece to finish the earrings.

Tip

Any of the projects in the metal clay section can be created using different types of clay. For example, the projects using low-fire silver clay can be created using standard-fire silver clay or even bronze clay. The primary differences between any of the clays are how the pieces are fired.

POLYMER CLAY

The creative possibilities seem endless when it comes to a medium like polymer clay, a molding product that must be cured in an oven after forming in order to harden. There is a plethora of clays and related products, which only adds more options for the polymer clay artist. The Art and Craft Materials Institute has determined that polymer clay is a nontoxic material, so it is safe to use in the home and even around children as long as it is not ingested, which is one reason it has become such a popular craft item for jewelry and other hobbies. Many of the tools used are also readily available in the home; however, even though polymer clay is not toxic, it is always a safe practice to work in a well-ventilated area and to use tools and other multifunctional items dedicated to the craft of polymer clay.

Tools and Supplies

Tools that help cut, shape, form, and bake polymer clay are helpful when working with this medium. Some of these might be found around the house already. Others you may have to buy specifically for this purpose. If you do use items from the home, such as a pie pan, it is best not to use them again for food after using them for clay, so consider this before raiding your pantry. Many of the tools, luckily, are not that expensive if you need to purchase them.

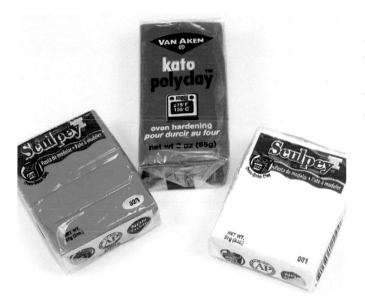

Polymer Clay: This moldable medium is a combination of polyvinyl chloride (PVC) and plastic additives that turns the PVC into a more elastic substance. There are a number of manufacturers of polymer clay, and that means there are lots of different types of polymer clay products available, such as Sculpey, Premo!, and Kato.

Mold Maker: There are a few mold-making brands on the market. Sculpey Mold Maker is one brand specifically designed to help create flexible molds for forming polymer clay.

Corn Starch: Regular corn starch keeps molds and stamps from sticking to polymer clay.

Polyblade: A long, sharp blade, much longer than a normal razor blade, a polyblade is designed specifically for cutting large chunks of polymer clay.

Craft Knife: For smaller or finer cutting, a regular craft knife is fine to use.

Acrylic Roller: To roll the clay into flat sheets, an acrylic roller is necessary. Acrylic will not stick to polymer clay.

Pasta Machine: While a pasta machine is not at all necessary for conditioning clay or rolling it flat, many polymer clay artists like to use one to help make the process faster and easier. These are the same types of machines used to make pasta, but they are often available at craft stores as well. Just make sure to only use it for polymer clay.

Wire and Pie Pan: For round objects such as polymer clay beads, insert a wire through the clay and balance the wire across a pie pan in order to keep the beads hanging so that the sides don't flatten.

Texture Plates and Stamps: Metal plates with various textures impressed into the plates work well for creating textures on polymer clay. These are specialty tools sold by craft supply vendors. Regular rubber stamps, the kind normally used for paper crafting, can also be used with polymer clay.

Ruler: To help ensure polymer clay sections are cut and formed into regular shapes, use a ruler to measure out the clay while you work with it.

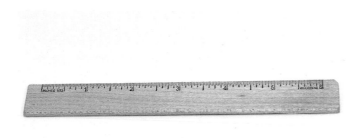

Piercing Tool: An awl, thick wire, or even a nail can work as a piercing tool when piercing holes through clay.

Wet Sandpaper: After baking, polymer clay will have a matte finish to it. However, you can give it a high shine by using wet 400- and 800-grit sandpaper.

Soft Cotton Cloth and Paper Towels: Use these for cleaning off polymer clay pieces after finishing them with wet sandpaper.

Parchment Paper and Baking Sheet: Because polymer is cured in a regular kitchen oven or toaster oven, parchment paper on a baking sheet or a polymer clay–dedicated baking sheet is necessary for placing flat items when they are ready to bake.

Oven: When polymer clay items are ready to cure, the next step is to bake them. The oven in your kitchen will work just fine if you plan to only bake polymer clay items occasionally; however, most serious polymer clay artists will use a small toaster oven that is dedicated to baking polymer clay.

Future Floor Finish and Small Brush: While there are a number of commercial products designed to help protect and finish baked polymer clay items, many polymer clay artists have found that Future floor wax applied with a small paintbrush works just as well.

Mixed-Media Inclusions: Acrylic paints, metal leaf, resin, mica powders, and other crafting supplies create all kinds of effects on polymer clay.

Techniques

There is no end to the techniques possible with polymer clay, but there are a few that are essential to getting started successfully as well as creating jewelry components. This techniques section covers some of the more important methods, such as conditioning, and some of the more creative methods, such as constructing and using molds. Because of the versatility of polymer clay, the techniques are extensive, and this section focuses on some of the more popular methods for making jewelry components such as beads, cabochons, and pendants. Polymer clay components combine well with other jewelry techniques such as bead stringing and wirework.

CONDITIONING CLAY BY HAND

Polymer clay comes in blocks that must be softened and conditioned before other techniques, such as rolling and cutting, can begin. It is always necessary to condition new clay before working with it. Even some of the softer types of polymer clay require conditioning for at least a few minutes. This can be done by either running the clay through a pasta machine or working it with your hands.

1 Always work over a nonstick surface, such as parchment paper.

2 Remove the protective wrapper from the clay, and roll the piece between your hands for a few minutes in order to warm the clay.

3 Continue to roll the clay into a long tube shape, fold the clay piece in half, and twist the two sides together.

4 Repeat step 3 a number of times until the clay feels soft and elastic.

YOU WILL NEED

• polymer clay

• parchment paper or other nonstick surface

3

Tip

Use this same conditioning technique to mix different colors of clay, either partially in order to form marbled patterns or completely to form new colors. It is best to work with lighter colors first and move toward darker colors to avoid staining lighter-colored clays.

ROLLING AN EVEN LOG

Logs of polymer clay can be used for anything from creating layers of different colors of clay (known as canes) or for twisting different colors of clay together, similar to the layers of a rope. In fact, polymer clay logs are also sometimes referred to as ropes or snakes. The trick is to get these logs as evenly shaped in diameter as possible, and not surprisingly, this can take some practice.

YOU WILL NEED

• polymer clay

• parchment paper

• scrap of cardboard or other nonstick surface

1 Condition the polymer clay, and select the amount you want to form into a log.

2 Place the clay on a nonstick surface, and use the palm of your hand to start rolling the clay piece back and forth until it becomes shaped like a log or long cylinder.

3 While rolling, concentrate on evening out the low and high spots of the log so that the log is the same diameter from one end to the other.

4 Once you get the log to the approximate size you want, take a piece of scrap cardboard, and place it on the log.

5 Place your hand on top of the cardboard without pressing down too hard, and roll the log back and forth a little more. This will help to remove any fingerprints that might have marked the clay.

Tip

If you are going to layer different colors of clay, start with flat pieces of clay that you have either rolled with an acrylic roller or through a pasta machine. Stack these on top of each other, and then roll them together into one large log. Then use the Rolling an Even Log technique to compact these together into one evenly shaped log of clay.

MAKING ROUND BEADS

Beads come in lots of different shapes, but the most common shape is round. Shaping polymer clay into round beads seems like a pretty simple task, but there are little tricks and techniques to centering the hole and keeping the beads round through the curing process.

1 Condition the clay, form the clay into an even log, and place this on a nonstick surface.

2 Use a ruler and a polyblade to section off equal amounts of the log.

3 Holding a small section of clay between the palms of your hands, lightly roll it in a circular motion until it is round.

4 Check occasionally as you roll it to see if it is round enough, and if not, reposition it between your palms and try it again. Like forming an even log, this can take some practice.

5 Once you have a round piece of polymer clay, use a piercing tool and twist it through the bead from one side until you just start to see the tip emerging.

6 Untwist the piercing tool from the bead and repeat step 5 from the other side, inserting the tool where it made the mark from the other side.

7 Insert the wire (which should be the same or smaller in diameter than the piercing tool) through the holes in the beads.

YOU WILL NEED

- polymer clay
- parchment paper or other nonstick surface
- ruler
- polyblade
- piercing tool
- wire
- pie pan
- oven

8 Place the wire over a pie pan while curing or baking using the polymer clay manufacturer's instructions. This will ensure that one side of the beads is not flattened, which can happen if placed on a flat surface when baking.

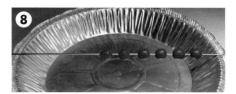

ROLLING AN EVEN SLAB

Flat pieces of clay, or slabs, are used to mix and layer colors of clay, so rolling an even slab of clay is a basic technique for the polymer clay artist. Slabs are usually placed one on top of the other in order to create canes of clay as well as filigrana logs, which have stripes of colored clay running through them. This is another technique that works well with a pasta machine, but it is also not that difficult to do with a few hand tools.

YOU WILL NEED

- polymer clay
- parchment paper or other nonstick surface
- acrylic roller
- two 2–3-mm skewers or popsicle sticks

1 Place the clay on the nonstick surface, and set one stick on either side of the clay.

2 Roll the acrylic roller over the sticks and clay. (This will help make sure the thickness stays even as you roll.)

3 Though this is not strictly necessary, you can square off the sides of the slab with a ruler and polyblade.

Tip

An even number of playing cards stacked on either side of the clay is an alternative way to make sure the thickness stays the same as you roll out the clay.

TEXTURING

Because of polymer clay's malleability, it is a wonderful material to create unique textures on, and it is pretty easy to do as well. Plus, if it doesn't turn out like you expected, you can just roll it up and start over again. Specialty plates are available from many polymer clay vendors; however, you don't need special tools to add texture. A number of household or natural items can be used make the clay surface more interesting.

YOU WILL NEED

- polymer clay
- parchment paper or other nonstick surface
- acrylic roller
- corn starch
- choice of texture plate

Tip

A similar technique can be used with rubber stamps. Just condition and roll out the polymer clay, coat the stamp with corn starch, and press it into the clay.

1 Condition clay and place it on a nonstick surface.

2 Roll out an evenly thick slab of polymer clay.

3 Sprinkle a small amount of corn starch on the texture plate.

4 Place the plate on top of the clay, use an acrylic roller to roll over the plate, and pull up the plate when finished.

PAINTING ON POLYMER CLAY

Painting on polymer clay is a way to add color and sparkle to cabochons or other elements formed with the clay. Most water-based paints and similar media, such as acrylic paints, work fine for painting on the surface of the clay. Avoid using oil-based products because they can melt the clay. It is even possible to create your own paints with some mica powder and plain acrylic medium or a product such as Translucent Liquid Sculpey, which is polymer clay.

YOU WILL NEED

- polymer clay
- parchment paper or other nonstick surface
- Translucent Liquid Sculpey
- mica powder (such as Pearl Ex)
- paintbrush
- small shallow bowl
- disposable mixing stick (such as a popsicle stick)

consistency you want. Just mix up what you will need for the amount of clay you plan to paint. There is no wrong way to do this since it all depends on your personal taste.

3 Once you have the amount of mica paint you want, use a small paintbrush to brush it over the clay component.

4 Allow the paint to dry thoroughly before baking the clay per manufacturer's directions. (If you are using acrylic medium, the clay should be baked first and then the piece painted, with no additional baking required. Translucent Liquid Sculpey requires that the piece is baked twice.)

1 Condition and form the polymer clay into whatever you are planning to make such as a cabochon or other component.

2 Add a few drops of mica powder to a small amount of acrylic medium in a small shallow bowl and mix the two together until you have the

MAKING AND USING MOLDS

While it is possible to purchase commercially available molds to use with polymer clay, it is not that difficult to make molds. You can use old scraps of leftover clay to form molds, or you can also use special products created for mold making. One product called Super Elasticlay MoldMaker makes flexible molds that enable the molded polymer clay to pop out easily, and once made, you can use the mold over and over again. When selecting objects to form molds with, try to use items that are flat on one side. Otherwise, you will have to reconstruct your piece after removing it from the mold. Some possible objects to use are refrigerator magnets and old jewelry pieces, such as pins and post or clip-on earrings.

YOU WILL NEED

- Super Elasticlay MoldMaker
- mold object
- polymer clay
- parchment paper or other nonstick surface
- corn starch

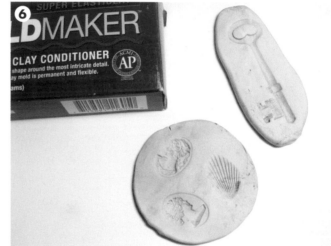

1 Condition and press out a thick slab of the mold maker.

2 Dust the surface of the mold maker and the object you want to make a mold of with corn starch (talcum powder also works) and press the object into the mold maker.

3 Carefully remove the object and bake the mold.

4 Condition regular polymer clay, and brush the mold with corn starch again.

5 Guide the clay into the small details of the mold first, and then fill the body of the mold with the rest.

6 Carefully remove the polymer clay cast from the mold and bake the clay following manufacturer's instructions.

FINISHING PIECES

After polymer clay pieces have been baked, a few more steps are necessary to give them a nice finish and a little protection. Finishing polymer clay pieces can be done with fancy tools (such as a felt buffing wheel) or a few simple hand tools. The hand tools may take a little longer, but the results are still excellent and a good way to start for the beginning polymer clay artist. Wet/dry sandpaper is best to use if you are after a high-gloss finish.

YOU WILL NEED

- 400-grit wet/dry sandpaper
- 600-grit wet/dry sandpaper
- 800-grit wet/dry sandpaper
- water and sink
- soft paper towel
- cotton cloth
- Future liquid floor polish
- small brush

2

4

1

1 Under lightly running water, sand the baked polymer clay piece with wet/dry 400-grit sandpaper, followed by 600-grit and then 800-grit paper.

2 Hand-buff the clay with a soft paper towel followed by a cotton cloth.

3 For an optional step in order to get a really superior finish, bake the piece again briefly at this point and then rub again with the cotton cloth.

4 Use a brush to apply Future floor polish and allow the clay piece to dry thoroughly before handling it again. The floor polish will give it some shine and help it resist scratching.

Projects

Now it is time to roll, form, press, and enjoy making polymer clay jewelry. These four projects show how it is possible to create some amazing jewelry designs with a handful of essential and creative polymer clay techniques. Jewelry designer and mixed-media artist Cyndi Lavin is responsible for infusing these projects with her own artistic perspective while still keeping them accessible for beginners.

POLY POLKA DOT EARRINGS

Earrings are just one of many jewelry pieces you can create after forming a cane of polymer clay. The flirty polka dot beads that are the focus of these earrings incorporate a number of techniques: Conditioning, Rolling an Even Log, Making a Round Bead, Rolling a Slab, and Finishing.

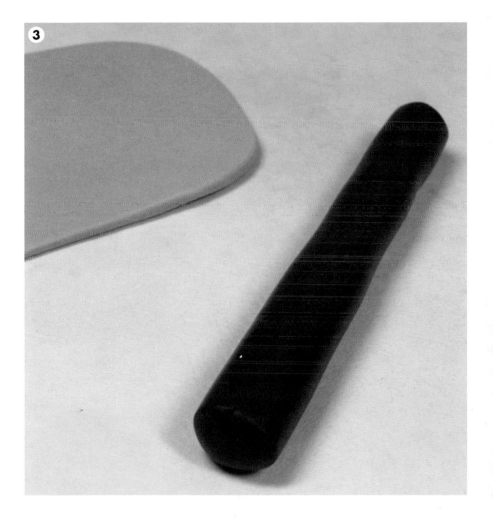

3

YOU WILL NEED

- Sculpey III in purple and spring lilac colors
- parchment paper or other nonstick surface
- acrylic roller
- ruler
- polyblade
- piercing tool
- wire
- pie pan
- oven
- lever backs
- head pins
- two purple glass flower beads
- two yellow size 11 seed beads
- two purple ceramic 4-mm beads
- round-nose pliers
- chain-nose pliers
- wire cutters
- 400-, 600-, and 800-grit wet/dry sandpaper
- paper towels
- cotton cloth
- Future floor wax
- small brush

1 After conditioning the clay, form and bake two beads that are about 10 mm in diameter (use the Making Round Beads technique, page 181). Do not worry about finishing these beads at this point.

2 Condition more purple clay and also some lilac-colored clay.

3 Make a 2-mm-thick slab using lilac clay, and roll an 8-mm-thick log using purple clay.

(continued)

4 Form these into a clay cane by wrapping the lilac clay slab around the purple log, and use a polyblade to trim the ends of the log evenly. Refrigerate the cane for a while to help keep it firm.

5 Slice eight thin pieces from the log with the polyblade.

6 Apply four slices to each of the baked round beads previously made, bake the beads again, and finish the surface of the beads.

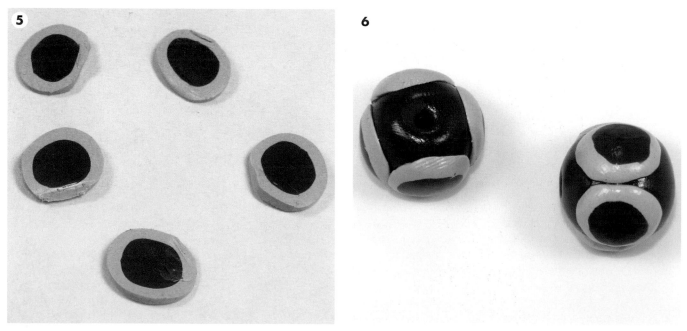

7

8

7 Gather the jewelry findings and accent beads for assembling the earrings. Stack one yellow bead, one flower bead, one of the polymer clay beads just made, and one purple bead onto a head pin.

8 Use chain-nose and round-nose pliers to form an unwrapped loop (page 46) at the top of the head pin. Use wire cutters to trim off excess head pin.

9 Slip a lever-back earring finding onto the loop at the top of the head pin.

10 Repeat steps 7 through 9 to assemble the second earring.

FILIGRANA HOOP EARRINGS

The effect known as filigrana is used in all types of artwork from paper to glass and, of course, polymer clay. The idea is to twist strands of colored material together so that it has an angled and striped effect. By twisting and rolling colorful canes of clay, you can create wonderful components that include this effect. For these filigrana beads that easily transform into earrings, you will use the following polymer clay techniques: Conditioning, Rolling an Even Log, Making a Round Bead, Rolling a Slab, and Finishing.

1 Condition the clay, and using an acrylic roller and sticks, roll out one blue, one purple, and two lilac clay slabs.

2 Stack the slabs in the following order: lilac, blue, lilac, purple.

(continued)

YOU WILL NEED

- Sculpey III in purple, spring lilac, and blue
- parchment paper or other nonstick surface
- acrylic roller
- two 23-mm skewers
- ruler
- polyblade
- piercing tool
- wire
- pie pan
- oven
- one pair of 1" (2.5 cm) gold-filled wire ear hoops
- 400-, 600-, and 800-grit wet/dry sandpaper
- paper towels
- cotton cloth
- Future floor wax
- small brush

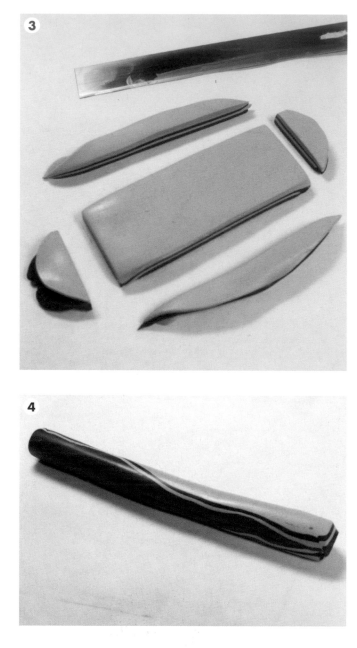

3 Cut off the edges to create an even rectangle.

4 Roll the stack into a log.

5 Alternately twist and roll the log (A), and eventually, you'll end up with a thinner and longer clay cane with various stripes of color (B).

6 Cut the log into 2⅜" (6 cm) sections.

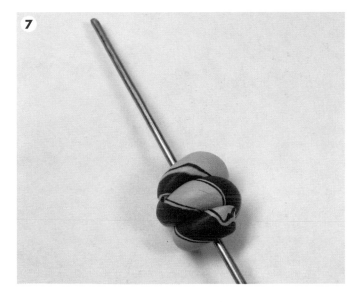

7 Wrap the clay sections around a wire and gently squeeze the clay together on the wire.

8 Suspend beads over a pie pan and bake.

9 Finish the surface of the beads, and allow them to dry completely before continuing.

10 Open the earring hoops, and slip a bead onto each one to create the earrings.

10

YOU WILL NEED

- Sculpey III in black
- parchment paper or other nonstick surface
- acrylic roller
- ruler
- polyblade
- craft knife
- texture plate
- two-part epoxy resin
- bone folder
- corn starch
- oven
- copyright-free color image of a lady, about 1½" (3.8 cm) in diameter
- two 10" (25.4cm) pieces of 0.5-mm link chain
- four 6-mm silver jump rings
- two 6-mm silver split rings
- one 6-mm silver spring ring clasp
- chain-nose pliers
- 400-, 600-, and 800-grit wet/dry sandpaper
- paper towels
- cotton cloth
- Future floor wax
- small brush

PRETTY LADY CLAY AND RESIN NECKLACE

Polymer clay, resin, paper, and chain are all combined in this necklace, a visual as well as tactile feast for the creative senses. Techniques used include Conditioning, Rolling an Even Log, Rolling a Slab, Texturing, and Finishing. It's amazing to discover how a little bit of texturing and a color image can transform simple black polymer clay.

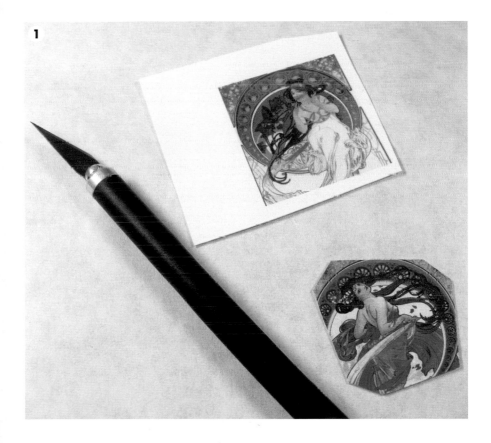

1 Cut out the image that you want to use. It can either be printed on a color printer or cut from a book, but make sure is copyright free.

(continued)

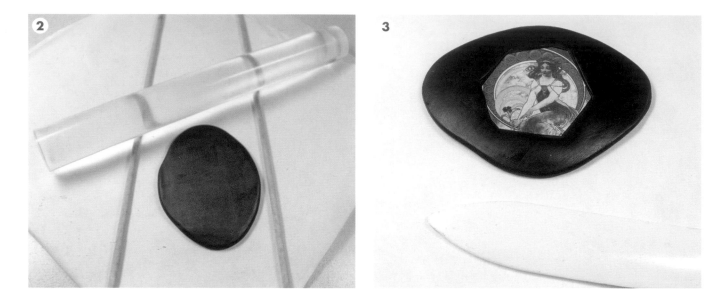

2 Condition the clay and roll an even slab approximately 2-mm thick.

3 Use a softly rounded tool such as a bone folder (or even a spoon) to push the image down into the clay, forming a shallow well.

4 Sprinkle corn starch on the texture plate, place the plate on the clay, roll over it with an acrylic roller, and pull up the plate.

5 Use a polyblade to cut around the clay and form an asymmetrical frame of clay around the image, removing excess clay.

6

8

10

6 With a craft knife, cut small slits on either side of the clay frame and insert jump rings in the upper edges.

7 Smooth the clay over the slits to close, and bake the clay per manufacturer's instructions (The low temperature will not harm most images, but if you think it might, you can remove the image before baking and then replace it for the next step.)

8 Mix two-part epoxy resin following the manufacturer's instructions. Pour resin over the picture, filling the well. Allow it to cure overnight.

9 Finish the clay with Future floor finish, and allow it to dry thoroughly before proceeding.

10 Attach a jump ring to one end of each chain section, and connect one of these jump rings to a spring ring clasp.

11 Attach the chains to the jump rings that are now baked into the clay frame using two split rings.

VINTAGE GARDEN GODDESS MOLDED PIN

Vintage or antique jewelry pieces can be reborn into new jewelry designs by using them to create molds. This particular pin was made using a cherished vintage pin from Cyndi Lavin's personal collection, but the motif, a mixture of a woman's face and natural elements such as fruit and leaves, is a familiar one from the Art Nouveau period.

2

3

YOU WILL NEED

- Sculpey MoldMaker
- corn starch
- Sculpey III in vanilla cream
- parchment paper or other nonstick surface
- antique jewelry piece
- oven
- 1½" (3.8 cm) pin back
- 400-, 600-, and 800-grit wet/dry sandpaper
- paper towels
- cotton cloth
- Future floor wax
- small brush
- Translucent Liquid Sculpey
- green, blue, purple, and bronze mica powders
- paintbrush
- small shallow bowl
- disposable mixing stick (such as a popsicle stick)
- black acrylic paint

1 Condition and press out a thick slab of MoldMaker.

2 Dust the surface of the MoldMaker clay and the object with cornstarch and press into the clay. Carefully remove the object and bake the mold. Allow to cool

3 Condition the polymer clay, dust the mold with cornstarch, and press polymer clay into the mold, starting with the deepest points.

(continued)

4 Carefully remove the cast polymer clay from the mold and bake the clay per the manufacturer's instructions.

5 Mix Liquid Sculpey with the various colors of mica powders to create the paints.

6 Paint the surface of the clay, green for the leaves, purple and blue for the fruit, blue for the eyes, and bronze for the face and background areas.

7 Bake the piece again for about 10 to 15 minutes, and allow it to cool.

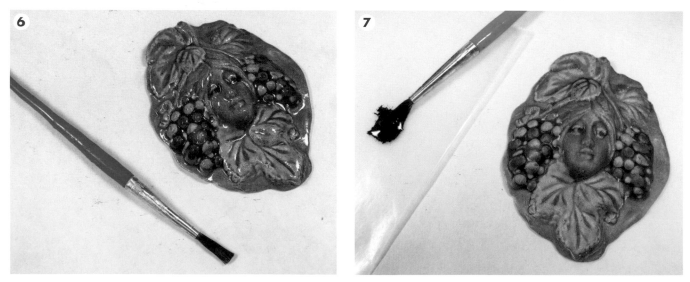

8

8. Apply black acrylic paint, wipe, and rinse it off. This will create an aged look to the finished piece. Repeat this multiple times until satisfied with the results.

9 Paint the back with black acrylic paint, and mix up a small amount of two-part epoxy resin to adhere the pin back (A). Allow the resin to dry completely before wearing the finished pin (B).

9A

9B

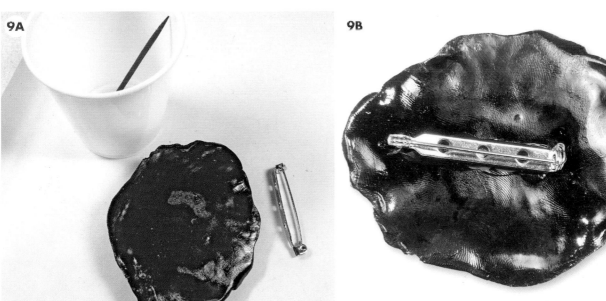

FIBER

Hemp, ribbon, linen cord, and felt are not typically considered jewelry-making materials, but fibers like these, as well as many other varieties, can either add to other jewelry-making methods, or they can stand alone as the main component of a design. Fiber is an excellent way to add texture and color that is not necessarily available with traditional jewelry-making materials such as metal or wire. This section examines a few different fiber jewelry techniques. Some, such as macramé knotting, may be familiar. Then there are techniques like basic crochet stitches that are normally used to stitch together fabric pieces, but there is no reason to limit fiber work to clothing.

Tools and Supplies

One big plus to using fiber to make jewelry is that it is fairly inexpensive and often materials can be recycled from other items. Save ribbons from gift boxes or other decorative items that otherwise might be thrown out. Most craft stores carry ribbon as well as hemp and other cording, and the cost is minimal. Other than the fiber items, only a few tools are needed, and again, many of these may be already found in the home or for a reasonable price at a craft or discount store.

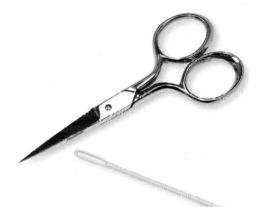

FIBER TOOLS

Scissors: A sharp pair of scissors is important to trim and cut fiber pieces. Make sure to dedicate these scissors to just fiber, and do not cut other items, such as paper, as this will dull the blades.

Large Needles: To weave in fiber ends and insert fiber through various components, large needles are helpful. Sometimes these are referred to as yarn needles, and they come in various diameters in both metal and plastic.

Crochet Hooks: Small crochet hooks in sizes B, C, or D (2 to 3 mm) are best when using crochet stitches to create small fiber jewelry components. The smaller hook (teamed up with thin thread) is required in order to make small, lacelike pieces. The size is imprinted on the hook.

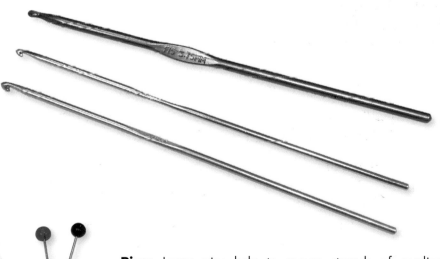

Pins: Large pins help to secure strands of cording. Quilting pins are available at most fabric stores and are longer than normal sewing pins. T-pins (shaped like the letter T) are also useful, but quilting pins are easier to locate, a little less expensive, and work just as well for most fiber projects.

Liquid Media: There are a number of liquid-based products on the market that work well with fibers, such as clear-drying tacky glue and fabric glue. These are useful for securing pieces of fabric or finishing off ends. Liquid seam sealant is another product to consider using, especially when working with ribbon that can fray easily on the ends. To help make fiber pieces strong, fabric stiffening products are also available.

Bulletin Board: When knotting fiber, especially when working macramé-type knots, a small bulletin board is a good work surface. Use pins to secure fibers to the board as you work.

Rubber Bands or Twist Ties: Long strands of fiber may be required when forming lots of knots. To keep fiber strands from tangling, it is a good idea to roll the ends of long fiber strands and use either twist ties or rubber bands to hold them together as you work.

TYPES OF FIBER

Hemp: Industrial hemp is a natural material originating from the cannabis plant. It has great texture and strength, so it works well for making jewelry pieces that will be worn a lot. The natural, or tan, color is most common, but these days, hemp comes in all types of colors as well as thicknesses. Hemp is relatively inexpensive, so it is a good material to use for learning knotting techniques.

Linen Cord: Linen cord is another good choice for knotting and creating interesting necklace or bracelet straps. Often linen cord has a waxed coating on it that helps keep knots in place. The more common color of linen cord is brown or black, but it is also available in many other colors.

Ribbon: Collect scraps of ribbon for all kinds of fiber jewelry uses. Add them to mixed-media designs or simply use a pretty piece of ribbon and dangle a pendant from it to create a quick necklace.

Crochet Thread: A thin cord used for creating ornate crochet pieces, crochet thread is normally associated with doilies; however, it is also excellent for bead crochet or making small lacy jewelry components.

Techniques

Macramé is one of the first fiber methods that come to mind when considering fiber jewelry making, but just about any technique used for other fiber crafting such as sewing, knitting, or crochet can also be incorporated into jewelry making. This section covers a few techniques borrowed from macramé as well as some methods from crochet that you may not have considered using for jewelry designing.

OVERHAND KNOT

The standard overhand knot method is very practical and good for all types of fiber work. This knot secures strands of fibers together and also is useful for finishing off pieces.

YOU WILL NEED

• fiber of your choice (such as hemp or linen cord)

1 Start by crossing one end of the cord over the other to form a loop.

2 Bring one end of the cord through the loop formed in the previous step.

3 Pull both ends of the cord to tighten and form the overhand knot.

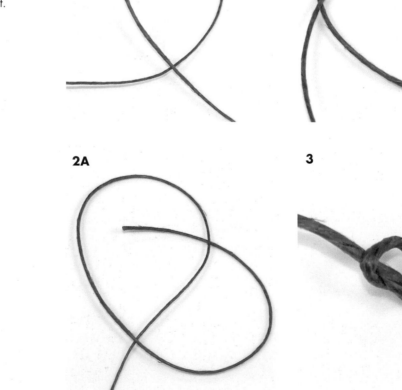

SQUARE KNOT

The square knot is another traditional knot used for many purposes and a basic knot for macramé jewelry. Multiple strands of cording must be used to complete a square knot, usually a minimum of three: one on the left side, one in the center, and one on the right side as you work. When square knots are completed successfully, the knots form a row of V shapes along the length of the cord.

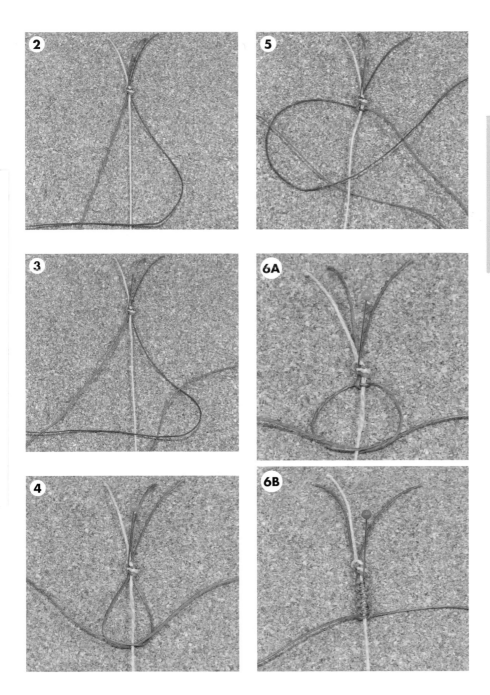

YOU WILL NEED

- fiber of your choice (such as hemp or linen cord)
- bulletin board
- pins

1 Secure all cords together at the top and pin them to a bulletin board. (An overhand knot works well for this).

2 Bring the right cord over the middle and left cords.

3 Bring the left cord under the middle cord and over the right cord.

4 Pull on both the right and left cords, pushing this part of the knot up against the top of the piece.

5 Repeat steps 2 through 4, but this time start with the left cord.

6 Continue working the square knot—right over left and then left over right (A)—until you get the desired length needed for your jewelry piece. As the piece gets longer, use pins to secure it in place on the board (B).

TWISTED HALF-KNOT

The twisted half-knot is really just the first half of a square knot. Because the knot is only created using one side of cording (working right over left) instead of working both sides of the cording (working right over left and then left over right), the knots automatically twist around.

YOU WILL NEED

• fiber of your choice (such as hemp or linen cord)
• bulletin board
• pins

1 Repeat steps 1 through 4 in the Square Knot instructions on page 207.

2 Continue to form knots—right over left—until you get the desired length needed for the jewelry piece. As the piece gets longer, use pins to secure it in place on the board.

Tip

Never stop a macramé project in the middle of a knot, as it can be confusing when you return to it.

CROCHET CHAIN STITCH

A chain doesn't have to be made out of metal. The chain stitch in crochet is a way to form a woven chain of fiber. It can either be used alone as a chain to dangle a pendant, or as the base into which more crochet stitches can be worked.

YOU WILL NEED

• crochet hook
• crochet thread

1
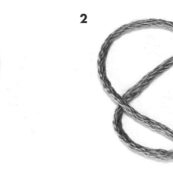

2

1 Attach the thread with a slip knot to the hook. To do this, make a loop of fiber by crossing one side of the thread over the other.

2 Then take the crossing thread in the previous step and place it under the thread loop, making sure to leave about a 6" (15 cm) tail of thread.

3 Insert the crochet hook under the crossing thread. Pull the tail and tighten the thread around the crochet hook.

4

5

6

4 Holding onto the thread tail, wrap the working thread counter clockwise around the hook.

5 Pull the hook down and through the loop of thread wrapped around the crochet hook. This forms the first chain stitch.

6 Repeat steps 4 and 5 until you have the desired number of chain stitches.

Tip

When learning to crochet, it is a good idea to use a larger hook and crochet thread (cotton yarn works well) so that you get the basics before using smaller hooks and thread to make jewelry components.

SINGLE CROCHET STITCH

Once a crochet chain is made, you can enlarge the piece by working more stitches into the chain. Single crochet is the easiest stitch to begin with.

YOU WILL NEED

- crochet hook
- crochet chain

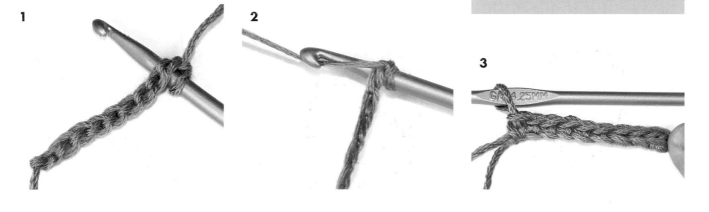

1

2

3

1 While holding onto the thread tail, insert the hook into the first chain from the hook.

2 Wrap the working thread around the hook, and use the hook to pull the thread through the chain stitch. This will make one single crochet stitch.

3 Continue to work single crochet stitches down the length of the chain.

SLIP STITCH

Sometimes it is necessary to join sections of crochet pieces together. One way to do this is with the slip stitch.

YOU WILL NEED

- crochet hook
- crochet chain

1 Insert the hook through the stitch you want the fiber piece to join.

1

2 Wrap the working thread over the hook.

3 Pull the working thread through the stitch as well as the second loop on the hook. There should just be one loop of thread on the hook when this stitch is completed successfully.

2

3

Tip

Make sure to keep about a 6" (15 cm) tail when working with most crochet or similar stitching techniques. Once a piece is finished, use a large needle to weave these tails back into the stitches.

BRAIDING

Just like braiding hair, this simple fiber technique requires at least three strands of fiber. However, you can also combine strands together as long as there are still three sections. This will make the finished braided piece thicker.

YOU WILL NEED

- fiber of your choice (such as hemp or linen cord)
- bulletin board
- pins

1 Start by separating the fiber into three sections, and use a pin to secure it to a work surface.

Tip

It is important to hold fiber strands tightly while braiding. Loose tension on the strands will make the finished braid loose as well.

2 Take the left outside strand and pull it over the center strand. That outside strand is now your center strand and the middle one moves to the outside.

3 Take the right outside strand and pull it over the middle strand. Now the right strand replaces the center strand.

4 Repeat steps 2 and 3 until you have the desired length of braid. As the piece gets longer, use pins to secure it in place on the board.

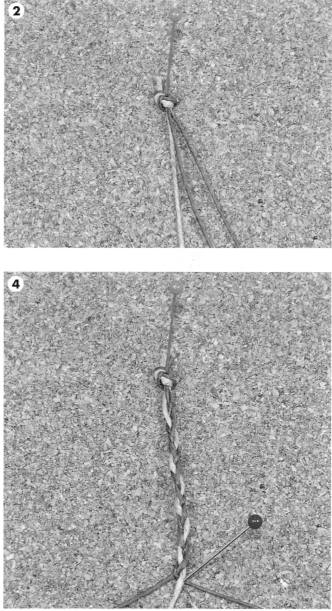

Projects

Hook, knot, twist, and stitch—it is time to start on some fiber jewelry. These projects give you a taste of various techniques that can easily be expanded on by adding more techniques or changing the types of fibers used.

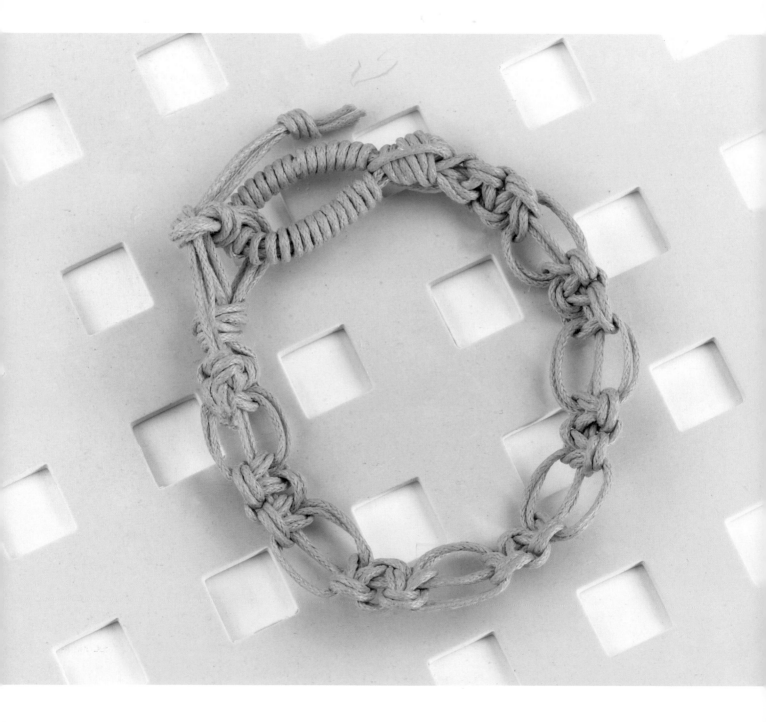

PEAK-A-BOO BLUE BRACELET

Leaving spaces between square knots creates a lacy look to this macramé bracelet, made of bright turquoise linen fiber. Simple knotting techniques including the Overhand and Square Knot are used in this bracelet project.

YOU WILL NEED

- three 36" (91 cm) strands of 1-mm turquoise waxed linen cord
- one 24" (60.9 cm) strand of 1-mm turquoise waxed linen cord
- scissors
- ruler
- bulletin board
- pins

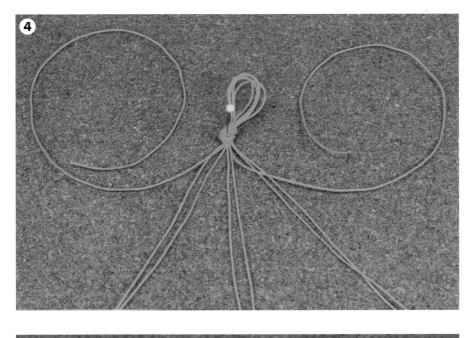

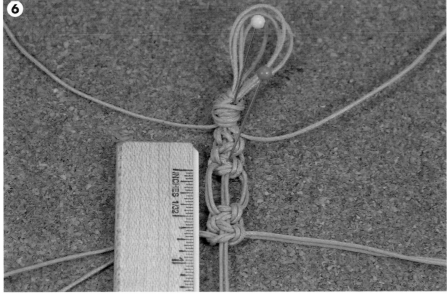

1 Line up the three longer strands of cord so their ends match, and fold them in half.

2 Fold the shorter strand in half, and place the center of that cord together with the longer strands so that all of them are folded in half.

3 Secure all of these together with an overhand knot about 1" (2.5 cm) from the folds. Pin the knot to a bulletin board.

4 Move the two shorter strands of cord above the overhand knot so they are out of the way, and separate the other strands into three sections that have two cords in each section.

5 Using the outside sections of cord, make two square knots (page 207).

6 Measure ½" (1.3 cm) down, and make two more square knots.

(continued)

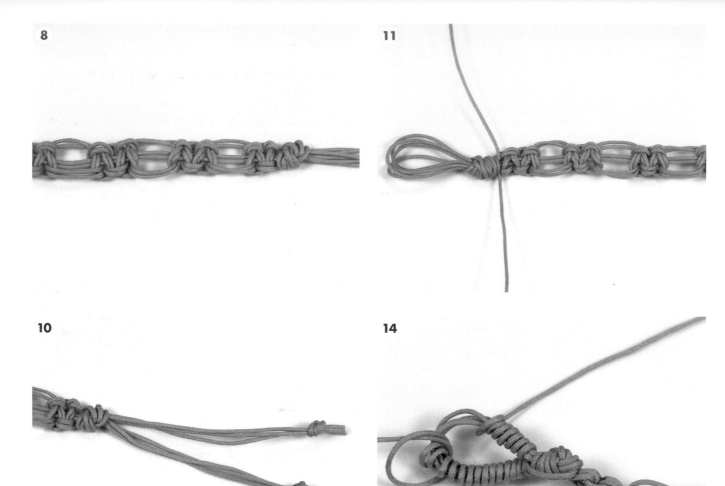

8

11

10

14

7 Repeat steps 5 and 6 until there are fourteen square knots and six spaces down the length of the bracelet.

8 After the last square knot, hold all six strands together and make an overhand knot.

9 Separate the strands into two sections with three strands each.

10 Measure about 2" (5 cm) down from the last knot and tie an overhand knot on each of the two sections, trimming off excess cord just past the knots. These ties will be used to close the bracelet.

11 Now start working on the other end of the bracelet, using the two shorter strands.

12 Beginning at the knot, wrap one strand around the cord loops up to the center of the loops.

13 Bring the end of the cord through one of the wraps to form a knot.

14 Start wrapping the other side of the loop with the other short cord in the same manner, catching the end of the first short cord under the last few wraps.

15

15 Bring the end of the second cord through one of the wraps to form a knot.

16 Knot the second cord again, and then trim off the excess cords.

17 To secure the bracelet to your wrist, knot the ties through the wrapped loop.

17

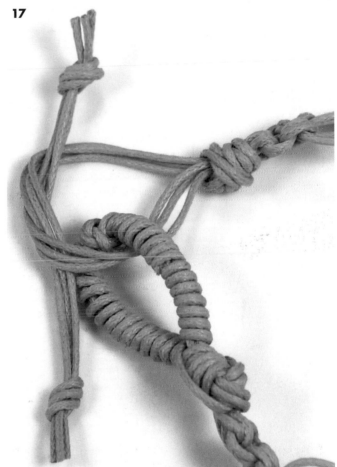

16

Tip

Anywhere from six to ten times the finished length is needed when estimating how much cord is needed to make a macramé piece. The number and types of knots will also affect the amount of cording required, so it is better to start with too much cord than too little.

DAY AT THE BEACH CHOKER

Hemp is tough and can really handle the elements, and for jewelry, that means wearing it frequently whether you are hanging out at the beach or at the office. This hemp choker has a shell dangling from the center and incorporates the Overhand and Twisted Half-knot techniques. Finished length is about 15" (38 cm). For a longer necklace, start with longer strands of hemp.

YOU WILL NEED

- three 9 ft. (2.7 m) strands of 1-mm hemp cord
- one shell with hole
- scissors
- ruler
- bulletin board
- pins
- twist ties or rubber bands
- glue
- one 8-mm jump ring
- chain-nose pliers

1

5

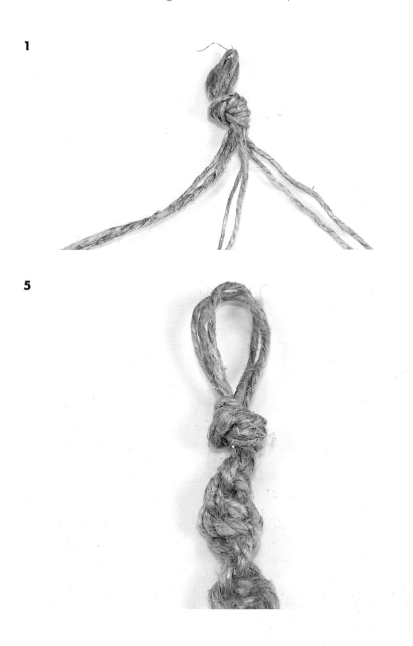

1 Align the three hemp strands, fold them in half, and tie them together in an overhand knot 1" (2.5 cm) below the folds.

2 Use pins to secure the knot to a bulletin board, and separate the strands into three sections with two strands of hemp in each section.

3 Roll up the ends of each cord section until you have about 12" (30 cm) of straight cord, and secure the rolled up cord with either twist ties or rubber bands. This will help to keep the hemp from tangling as you work.

4 Start making twisted half-knots (page 208), using the two outside cords to knot and keeping the center cords in the middle.

5 Work twisted half-knots until you have 12" (30 cm) of knots.

(continued)

6 Separate the strands into two sections with three strands in each, and tie a basic knot (right over left).

7 Apply clear-drying glue to the knot just formed. Allow the glue to dry before continuing.

8 Once the glue is dry, use scissors to trim off one of the cord sections, and make an overhand knot on the end of the other section of cord, trimming off any cord past the knot as necessary.

9 Open a jump ring and slip it into the hole of the shell.

7

8

10

10　Locate the center of the twisted half-knots, insert the jump ring around a strand of hemp, and use chain-nose pliers to close the jump ring.

11　To attach the choker, slip the straight cord section created in steps 6 to 8 through the hemp loop on the other end of the choker, and knot it around the loop.

Tip

Many shells picked up from the beach already have holes in them. These are perfect for jewelry since drilling a hole isn't required.

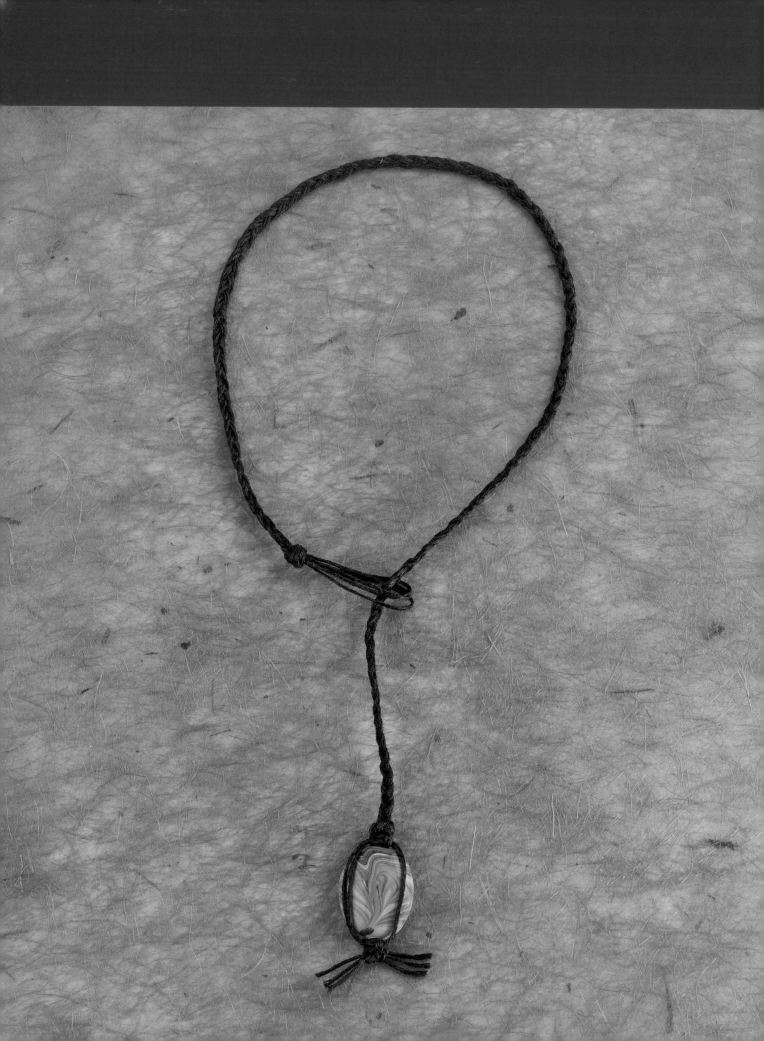

1

PAINTED DESERT BRAIDED LARIAT

The swirling earth-tone colors in the ceramic bead that is attached to the end of this lariat necklace were the inspiration for this design. It shows how one bead can start a design process. Fiber techniques include Braiding, Overhand Knots, and Square Knots.

1 Line up the three waxed linen strands so their ends match, fold them in half, and tie an overhand knot, leaving a loop of cord at least 1" (2.5 cm) long. This is important so that the bead can fit through it. (If you use a different-sized bead, make sure to double check that it will fit through the loop before tightening the overhand knot.)

(continued)

YOU WILL NEED

- three 4 ft. (1.23 m) strands of brown waxed linen cord
- one 25 × 18-mm ceramic bead
- scissors
- ruler
- bulletin board
- pins

2 Use pins to secure the knot to the bulletin board.

3 Separate the six strands into three sections, two strands each, and begin to braid the three sections of cord tightly. Continue until you have about 15" (38 cm) of braided cording.

4 With the two outside sections, tie a basic knot, right over left.

5 Then tie a square knot, again with the two outside sections of cords.

6 Add the bead to the center strands and push it up flush against the square knot.

7 Tie another square knot, positioning the cords on the sides of the bead so that two strands hug the front of the bead and two strands hug the back of the bead.

8 Take the two outside sections, and tie a basic knot, right over left.

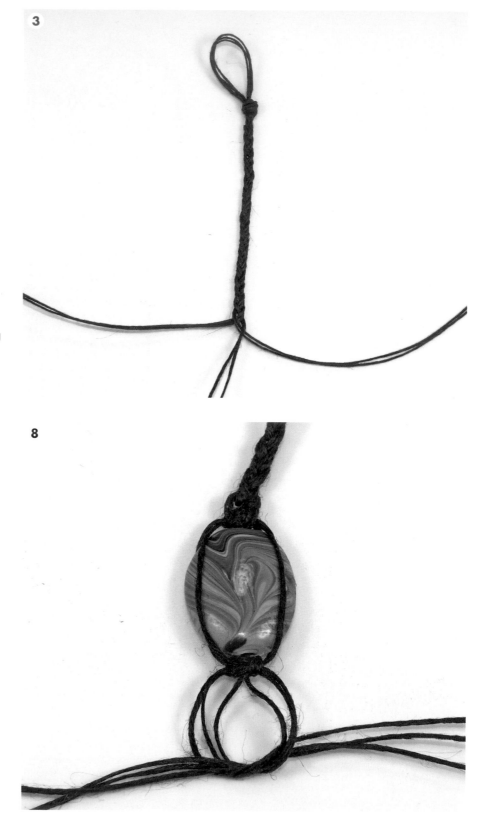

9

9 Use scissors to trim off cording below the knots, leaving ½" (1.3 cm) ends of cord.

10 To wear the lariat, just drape the braided cord around your neck and insert the bead through the loop on the end.

Tip

Don't forget to use pins to secure fiber pieces as you work on them. This will help keep tension tight.

10

GOLDEN CIRCLE CROCHET EARRINGS

A wonderful lacy look is achievable with the use of small crochet hooks and metallic crochet thread. It only requires a few basic crochet stitches—Chain Stitch, Slip Stitch, and Single Crochet—so even a beginner can find success. Finally, dangle a crystal bead from the fiber circles (using the Unwrapped Loop technique described in the Wire Work section, page 46) to add a little extra sparkle.

1 Attach thread to the crochet hook, leaving a 6" (15 cm) tail of thread, and make five chain stitches.

2 Connect both ends of the chain using a slip stitch.

(continued)

YOU WILL NEED

- metallic gold crochet thread
- 2.25-mm crochet hook
- yarn needle
- scissors
- two gold-filled ear hooks
- two 6-mm clear crystal beads
- two gold-tone head pins
- wire cutters
- round-nose pliers
- chain-nose pliers

3 Make one more chain stitch, and then make ten single crochet stitches inside the circle created in the previous step.

4 Connect both ends using a slip stitch.

5 Chain one and single crochet in each stitch around the circle created in the previous step.

6 Connect both ends using a slip stitch.

7 Chain one, make one single crochet in the next stitch, chain one, make one single crochet in the next stitch, and repeat this all around the circle (alternating between chain one and single crochet stitch).

3

5

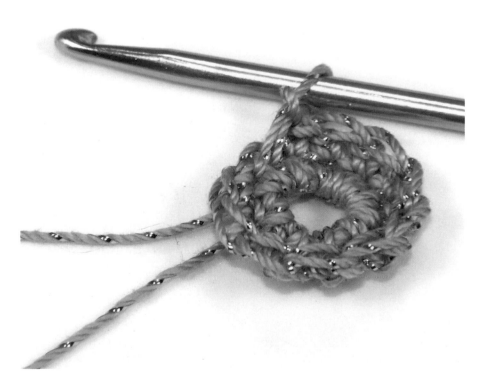

8

8 Finish off the circle using a slip stitch, leaving a 6" (15 cm) tail when you cut the thread. Pull the working thread completely through the remaining loop, and pull tight to secure.

9 Use a yarn needle to weave both tails into the finished circle a few times, and trim off excess thread.

10 Repeat the steps above to create a second crochet circle.

11 Put a crystal on a head pin, make an unwrapped loop on it, and attach this loop to any of the stitches along the outside of the crochet circle. Repeat this for the other circle.

12 Attach the loop of an ear hook to the edge of the crochet circle opposite the crystal dangle. Repeat this for the other crochet circle in order to complete the earrings.

12

1 Keeping the cotton thread on its spool, add a beading needle to the thread and string twenty-seven glass beads onto the thread, pushing the beads down as you go until there is about 12" (30 cm) of thread to work with.

2 Pull off the needle, and attach the thread to the crochet hook with a slip knot (page 208) leaving a 6" (15 cm) tail of thread.

3 Make two chain stitches on the thread.

4 Push one bead down against the last stitch.

5 Repeat steps 3 and 4 until all beads have been used.

6 Finish with two chain stitches.

7 Trim thread, leaving a 6" (15 cm) tail, and pull the end of the thread through the last chain to finish off the end.

DAINTY BEADED CROCHET BRACELET

Add beads to fiber as you crochet this dainty bracelet. This easy bracelet primarily uses the crochet chain stitch, and you just add a bead in between a few stitches as you go. To attach the bracelet to your wrist, tie both tails of thread into a bow.

1

3

4

5A

5B

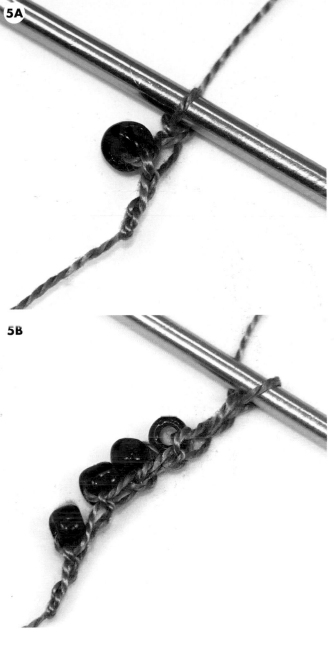

Tip

When first starting a crochet piece, hold onto the fiber tail with the hand that is not working with the crochet hook in order to keep tension even as you stitch.

RESIN

Also sometimes referred to as two-part epoxy, resin used for jewelry making is a synthetic material made up of a polymer product (the resin) and a hardening agent. Mixed together, they eventually turn solid and can be used for casting items, adhering elements together, or coating components. Resin products are widely available at most craft stores and also many home improvement or hardware stores. Prefabricated resin products in the form of beads, charms, and finished jewelry items are also available and very popular. Resin jewelry is lightweight, colorful, and fairly easy to make. When mixing resin products, make sure to follow all manufacturers' safety guidelines and work in a well-ventilated area.

Tools and Supplies

To make resin jewelry, only a few tools and supplies are necessary. In addition to resin, you will also need materials to help mix, set, and cast the resin.

Resin Products: There is a large variety of resin products on the market, and the type of resin product you use depends on a number of factors. For example, for casting, epoxy casting resin or polyurethane casting resin is necessary. For creating a top coat, epoxy coating resin is used. Adhesive resin normally comes in two parts that must be mixed together. Most hardware stores carry resin used for sticking items together. When in doubt, read the instructions on the box the resin comes in to determine if it is the right product for your jewelry project.

Molds: To form jewelry components such as resin cabochons, molds are perfect for casting. Ice cube trays can be used along with molds specifically designed for resin products.

Rotary Tool: A rotary tool, also used for polishing and chain making, is useful for drilling holes and also sanding resin components.

Sanding Attachment and Drill Bits: A sanding attachment that connects to a rotary tool will make sanding resin components very quick. Drill bits are necessary for creating holes in resin components so they can be connected to other elements such as jump rings.

Mold Release: Resin will stick in some molds if they are not first sprayed with a product called mold release, designed specifically for resin work.

Embossing Gun: An embossing gun is normally used by rubber stamp crafters, but it works really well for removing bubbles from liquid resin.

Resin Dye: Create all kinds of colorful effects with clear resin by adding resin dye. It comes in powder or liquid form as well as opaque or transparent colors.

Respirator and Gloves: Though resin doesn't usually have an obvious odor to it, repeated exposure can be harmful. Wear a respirator to protect your lungs. Wear disposable gloves when handling resin products as well.

Disposable Mixing Cups, Measuring Cups, and Stir Sticks: In its liquid form, resin is toxic, so it is necessary to use disposable cups and stir sticks when mixing resin products. Old plastic coffee scoops work well for disposable measuring cups. Otherwise, try to find clear plastic graduated measuring cups.

Waxed Paper: Resin is sticky stuff, so wax paper is helpful for covering work surfaces.

Miscellaneous Findings and Metal Blanks: In order to turn resin components into finished jewelry pieces, make sure to have a stash of standard jewelry findings on hand, such as jump rings, clasps, and ear hooks. Metal blanks for gluing on cabochons are also useful.

Hand Tools: General jewelry-making tools are needed to assemble jewelry pieces after the resin items are completed: chain-nose pliers, wire cutters, and round-nose pliers.

Dust Mask and Goggles: When sanding material such as resin, where dust mask and goggles to protect your eyes and lungs.

Tip

By law, resin product manufacturers are required to provide safety information on all their merchandise. Whenever using a resin product for the first time, read the instructions thoroughly before starting a project.

Techniques

Making jewelry using resin products is not complicated; it does require work with the material so that you know how it is supposed to look at various stages. The most difficult part of any resin jewelry making is waiting for it to cure! The techniques here cover the basics, but don't be afraid to create some of your own as you get to know this unusual medium. Like a mad scientist's mixing and measuring, pouring and covering, casting and drilling, the end result may turn into a very successful resin jewelry experiment.

MIXING RESIN

Always follow the manufacturer's instructions when mixing any resin product. However, most resins will require mixing two parts of a solution. The solution consists of resin and a hardener, each packaged in separate bottles.

4

YOU WILL NEED

- casting resin product
- disposable mixing cups
- disposable stir sticks
- gloves
- respirator
- wax paper

1 Cover a work surface with wax paper.

2 Measure out equal parts of the two part epoxy product (resin and hardener) in two separate cups.

3 Pour the hardener measured out directly into the resin cup, and start stirring. Don't stir too vigorously or air bubbles will form.

4 Continue to stir for about two minutes, making sure to scrape the sides occasionally to get all of it mixed well. Again refer to manufacturer's instructions.

5 At this point, the resin is ready to pour. It will be necessary to pour the resin fairly soon after mixing so that it won't set up in the mixing cup.

POURING RESIN FOR CASTING

Once the resin is mixed, it is time to pour it. To use resin for casting, pour it into a mold of some kind once the resin is mixed properly. It is a good idea to be ready to pour as soon as the resin is mixed since it starts to harden and cure soon after mixing.

1 Cover a work surface with wax paper.

2 Spray the mold with mold release, if necessary, and allow to dry before mixing resin. Mold release drying time can vary depending on the manufacturer and climate.

3 Once the mold release is dry and the resin has been thoroughly mixed, pour a little of it into the mold.

4 If adding decorative elements such as stickers, paper pieces, or beads, add those after pouring only half the resin.

5 Allow the decorative elements to settle, and pour the rest of the resin in the mold.

6 Set the mold in an area where the resin can thoroughly cure without being disturbed. Depending on the type of resin used and the temperature and size of the item, it can take anywhere from 24 to 72 hours for it to completely cure. Resin items should not be tacky to touch if cured properly.

YOU WILL NEED

- premixed casting resin product
- gloves
- mold release
- mold
- respirator
- wax paper

Tip

If bubbles show up after pouring resin, use an embossing gun and blow over the resin for a few minutes from about 6" (15 cm) or more away. Be careful not to blow too much or the resin can splash out of the mold. Also, if the heating element is too hot, it can melt plastic molds.

MAKING RESIN MOLDS

Though plenty of molds are available from basic ice cube trays to fancy molds made specifically for resin jewelry, it is also possible to make molds using silicone products.

YOU WILL NEED

- Castin' Craft EasyMold Silicone Rubber

- object to make mold

1 Choose a small object to make a mold from. Something without a lot of detail works best.

2 Following the instructions on the EasyMold product, take equal parts of the two putties and blend together until all marbling is gone.

3 Roll the putty into a ball and flatten into a thick pancake.

4 Press the object into the putty, wait for about 10 minutes, then pull the object out, and set the putty aside to dry.

5 In about 10 minutes, your mold should be ready.

Tip

If you aren't sure if the mold used requires mold release, test it by pouring a small amount of resin on the back of the mold someplace that won't affect the cavities in the mold. If it sticks, then that mold requires mold release. If it doesn't stick, then no mold release is necessary.

DYING RESIN

Experiment with color by dying resin.

YOU WILL NEED

- premixed casting resin product
- pigment liquid resin dye
- gloves
- respirator
- wax paper

1 Cover a work surface with wax paper.

2 Once the resin has been mixed, add a tiny drop of the liquid pigment into the cup of resin and mix with a stir stick.

3 If the color is as dark as you want, you can pour the resin; however, if you want a darker color, add another tiny drop and mix some more until you achieve the required color.

TOP COATING RESIN

Besides using resin for casting items, it is also useful for coating elements. For example, paper items or fabric can be coated with resin to create a protective and glossy finish.

YOU WILL NEED

- epoxy coating resin
- gloves
- respirator
- wax paper
- heat embossing gun

1 Cover a work surface with wax paper.

2 Mix the resin together.

3 Pour the resin mixture over the item to be coated making sure all edges are covered evenly.

4 Check for bubbles periodically as the item dries, and heat with an embossing gun for a few minutes to remove any bubbles.

5 Set the mold in an area where the resin can thoroughly cure without being disturbed.

DRILLING HOLES IN RESIN

One of the easiest ways to assemble resin components into jewelry is by connecting them with findings such as jump rings, but that means some of the resin components will need holes. This is accomplished with the use of a rotary tool and drill bit.

YOU WILL NEED

- resin component
- drill bit
- rotary tool
- scrap piece of wood
- dust mask and goggles

1 Place the resin component on a piece of wood, and hold it in place.

2 Attach a small drill bit to a rotary tool.

3 While holding the resin on the wood, drill a hole through the resin, stopping once the wood is pierced.

SANDING RESIN

To finish off any rough areas of resin, it may be necessary to sand parts of resin components, such as around the edges. A rotary tool comes in handy for this basic task.

YOU WILL NEED

- resin component
- sanding attachment
- rotary tool
- dust mask and goggles

1 Make sure the resin piece is completely cured before sanding.

2 Connect a sanding attachment to the rotary tool.

3 While holding the resin piece in one hand, run the attachment along the sides of the resin.

4 Repeat as necessary until all edges are smooth.

Projects

Now it is time to make some inspirational resin jewelry. The projects in this section are designed and demonstrated by Jennifer Perkins. Well-known for her fun and quirky jewelry pieces, Jennifer's ideas are very accessible, even for first-time resin jewelry makers, and there's no doubt you'll find loads of inspiration for creating your own resin designs as well. Brand names of Jennifer's favorite resin products have been included in the project instructions, and most of these are available in regular craft stores or through crafting supply web sites (see page 290).

Tip

Ice cube trays make great inexpensive resin molds. Plus, they usually don't require mold release, which is one extra step you can then skip while using them to cast resin. However, all ice cube trays are not created equal. Look for one with a perfectly square bottom that is made of somewhat flexible plastic. Grocery stores and thrift stores are good places to look. If you aren't sure if the resin will stick, test it out by adding a little resin to the back and seeing if it will come off after curing.

TIGER RING

This whooper of a ring, measuring around 1" by 1½" (2.5 × 3.8 cm), is fun and funky but also very adaptable. By selecting a different image to cast inside the resin, this ring design becomes totally different. Select an image that makes a statement. The image used in this ring was originally painted by Jennifer's sister, Hope Perkins. Resin techniques used include Mixing, Pouring, Dying, Sanding, and Adding a Top Coat.

1 Cover the work area with waxed paper.

2 Select an image, preferably one that is square, and use image editing software to size the image so that it will fit an ice cube slot in the tray.

3 Print the picture out onto glossy photo paper. (Regular printer paper is too thin.)

4 Cut out the image and round the edges slightly.

5 In a well ventilated area, mix equal parts Easy Cast Clear Casting Epoxy in a plastic cup. For the first batch, only a small amount of resin is needed.

6 Fill an ice cube cup about ¼" (6 mm) deep with the resin.

7 Allow the resin to set up and harden somewhat.

8 Mix more resin and pour a small amount of it on top of the hardened resin poured earlier.

(continued)

YOU WILL NEED

- ring blank
- ice cube tray
- photo quality printer paper
- printer
- computer
- scissors
- Easy Cast Clear Casting Epoxy
- rotary tool
- sanding attachment
- dust mask and goggles
- Castin' Craft Resin Spray
- image editing software
- Castin' Craft Opaque Blue Pigment
- mixing cups and stir sticks
- waxed paper

6

9

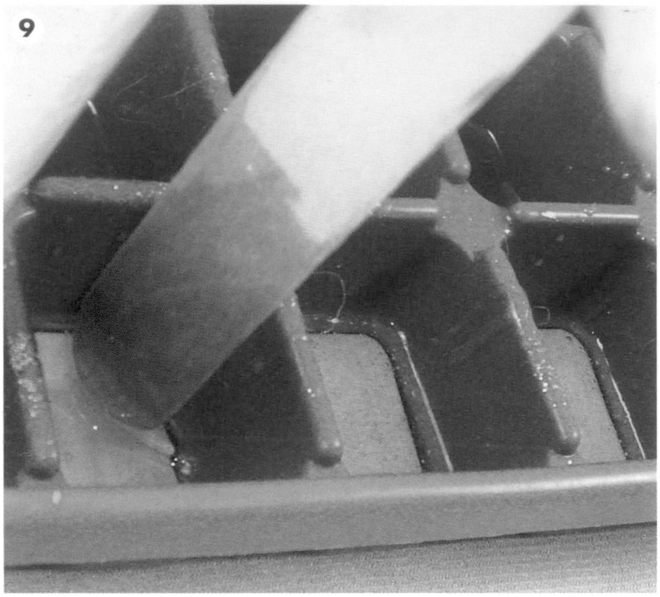

12

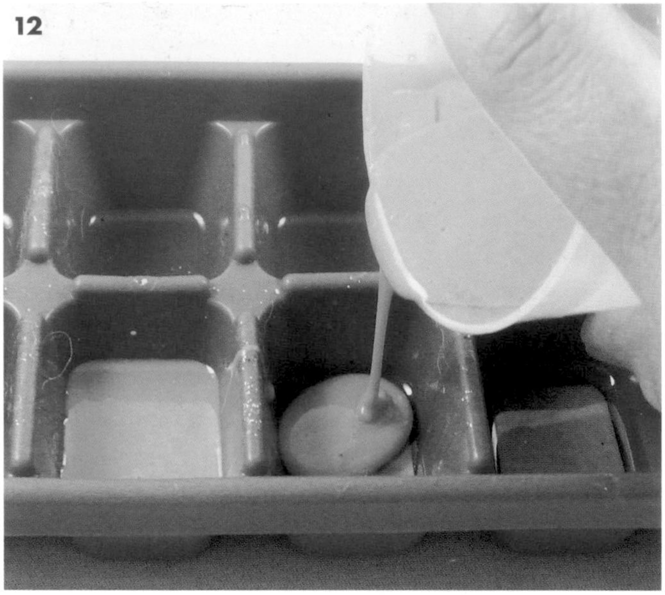

11

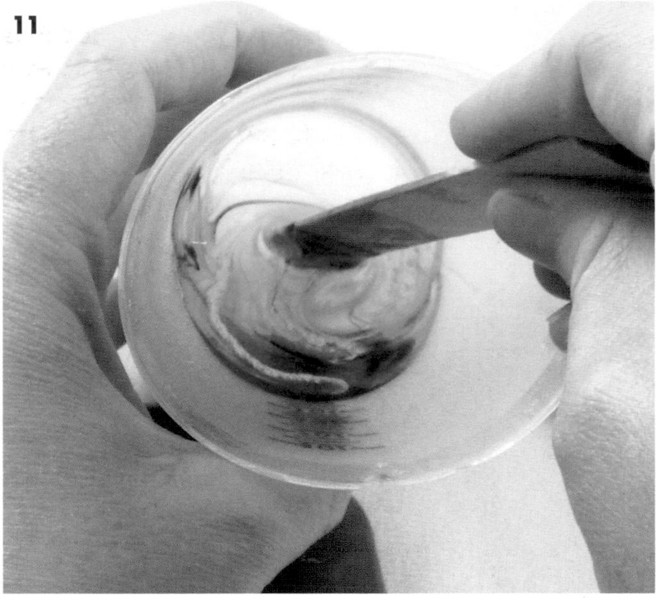

13

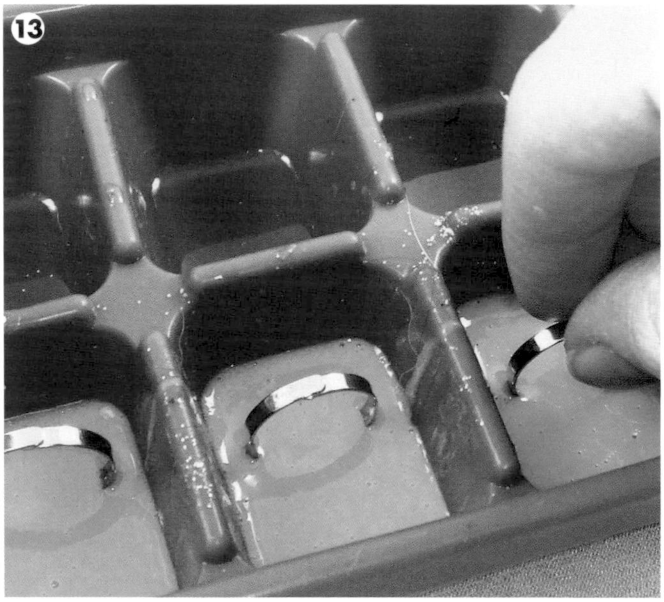

9 With the image facing down, place it in the wet resin. Using a stir stick, poke at the back of the image to help remove any bubbles. The resin should come from underneath the image and around the sides to completely cover the back side.

10 Allow the resin to harden a little before continuing.

11 When the resin has hardened slightly, mix more resin and add a tiny amount of dye (Castin' Craft Opaque Blue Pigment).

12 Pour a small amount of resin over the previously poured pieces (which will be the back side when removed from the mold).

13 Place the ring blank in the center of the cube, making sure that there is enough resin to cover the ring.

14 Allow the ring to harden for at least 24 hours.

15 When the resin has hardened (cured) completely, pop the ring out of the tray just like you would an ice cube.

16 Following the sanding technique (page 237) previously described, sand all the edges of the resin that is now attached to the ring.

17 Once the edges feel smooth to the touch, spray the ring with Castin' Craft Resin Spray. Allow the resin spray to dry completely before wearing the ring.

Tip

To add a little extra protection and shine to finished resin pieces, consider using a resin spray. Sometimes sanding can give resin a dull appearance, but adding a top coat of resin spray brings resin back to its full shine.

YOU WILL NEED

- Castin' Craft Opaque Pigment White
- Castin' Craft Opaque Pigment Blue
- Castin' Craft Clear Polyester Casting Resin
- Castin' Craft EasyMold silicone rubber
- Liquid Fusion Glue
- pin back
- object to make mold
- mixing cups and stir sticks
- waxed paper

VINTAGE RESIN BLUE BIRD PIN

Turn a favorite vintage piece of jewelry into a resin replica by first using a resin mold technique to transfer the original form into a mold. Then fill the mold with resin to cast a jewelry component that looks similar to the original piece. In this project, Jennifer used a cherished vintage bird pin to press into a mold she made from silicone rubber (as described in the Making Resin Molds technique, page 235). Then she used the Dying Resin technique (page 236) to color her resin blue to make a blue bird pin.

1 Following the Making Resin Molds technique, page 235, use EasyMold to mix up the mold putty, and select a vintage jewelry piece to replicate in the mold.

(continued)

1

2 Press the original vintage item into the putty, pull it out, and allow the mold to dry before continuing.

3 Mix the casting resin (A), and add blue and white opaque pigment to achieve a pastel color (B).

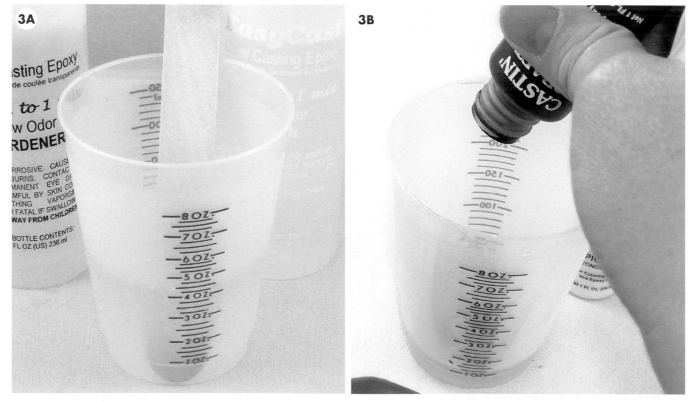

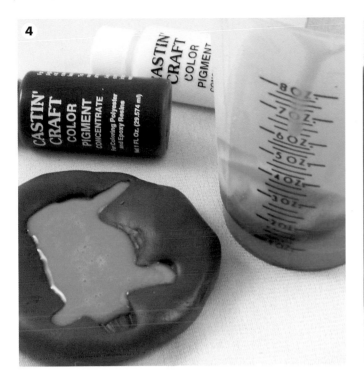

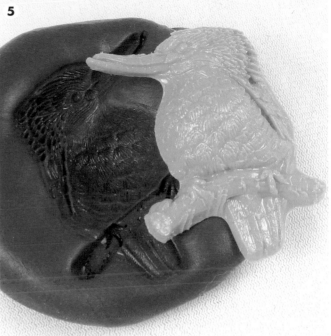

4 Pour the casting resin into the mold.

5 Allow the resin to set up for 24 hours before removing it from the mold.

6 Using a strong glue (such as Liquid Fusion), attach the pin back to the bird, and allow the glue to dry 24 hours.

WEAR YOUR COLLECTION NECKLACE

With this wonderful resin method designed by Jennifer Perkins, it is possible to turn 3D collectibles into portable mementos. The result is a whimsical necklace with original artwork as the focal point of the necklace. This necklace uses just about all of the resin techniques described in this section as well as techniques from Bead Stringing, page 24, and Chain Making, page 66, so it is a project for the more adventurous resin experimenter. However, the time and effort will be worth it when you have a one-of-a-kind piece of wearable art. Adobe Photoshop was used in the following steps, but any image-manipulation software can be used instead. There are some low-cost and freeware programs online.

1   Choose a few collectible items such as dolls or figurines, the brighter and more colorful the collectibles the better, and use a digital camera to take a picture of them. They need to show up well against the patterned paper background. (For the images used in Jennifer's necklace design, she chose to use the heads of animal figurines.)

2   Choose a patterned piece of paper, such as black and white polka dots, and use a computer scanner to scan the paper.

3   Bring up Photoshop, open the scan from step 2, select a 2" × 2" (5 × 5 cm) section of the scan at 300 dpi, and save this.

4   Next open each of the digital images taken in step 1, crop them as close to the sides of the images as possible, and make the width of each roughly ¾" (1.8 cm) in size and 300 dpi.

(continued)

YOU WILL NEED

- plastic painter's palette tray
- Castin' Craft Resin
- rotary tool
- sanding attachment
- 16-mm drill bit
- computer and scanner
- photograph quality paper
- printer
- collectible items
- patterned paper
- nine 10-mm jump rings
- flat-nose pliers
- hook-and-eye clasp
- four 2 × 2-mm sterling crimp beads
- beading wire
- digital camera
- Photoshop or other image editing software
- ink pen
- coin
- scissors
- eight 30-mm black beads
- eight 15-mm corrugated red plastic beads
- eighteen 4-mm plastic yellow beads
- top coat resin
- small piece of wood
- mixing cups and stir sticks
- waxed paper
- wire cutters
- Castin' Craft Resin Spray

5 In Photoshop, unlock the layers so that you can then use the magic wand tool to select and cut or delete the background.

6 While the animal image is open (which at this point should have a gray and white check background), open the 2" (5 cm) square of the background (created in step 3) at the same time so that the two images are side by side.

7 Use the Photoshop "move tool" to place the cutout animal images onto the black and white polka-dotted image, moving the images around until they are centered, and copy and paste the images side by side into a word processing document.

8 Use the photo quality and best quality settings on the printer, set the paper choice options to "other specialty" (papers in most cases), and select print.

9 Once the paper has been printed, use a coin (or other circular item such as the cabochon shown here) that is slightly smaller than the well in the painter's palette as a template.

10 Place the coin over the image, trace a circle around the coin, and use scissors to cut out the image. Four complete images (using steps 1 to 8) are needed.

11 Cover a work area with wax paper, mix some casting resin (A), and fill four spots in the painter's palette a third full (B).

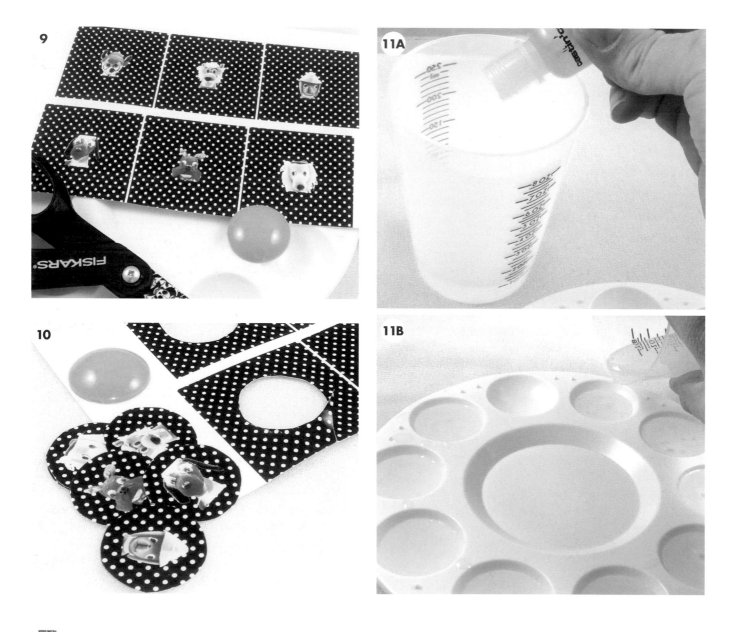

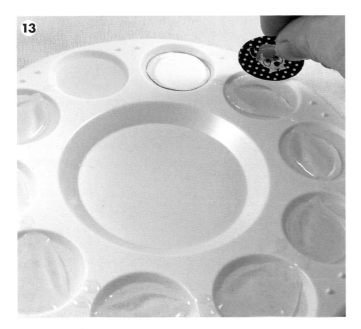

13

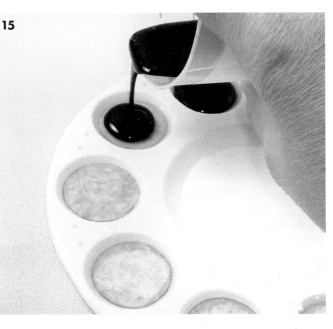

15

14

16

12 Once the first layer of resin has started to harden, pour the second layer of resin on these same four areas of the palette. This layer should fill them about two thirds.

13 Add the printed circle images face down into the resin.

14 Use a stir stick to poke the backs of the images in order to make sure all the bubbles are gone and that the resin comes around the sides and covers the backs of the images, and allow this resin to set up.

15 Mix a third batch of resin, add black resin dye to it, fill the rest of the well with the colored resin, and allow the resin to cure completely.

16 Once the resin is fully cured, pop out each resin cabochon from the palette mold.

(continued)

17 Sand the edges of each resin piece until it is smooth.

18 Drill a hole in either side of each resin cabochon.

19 Once each cabochon is sanded and drilled, spray it with a protective top coat of Castin' Craft Resin Spray on both sides, allowing it to dry completely.

20 To assemble the necklace, connect the resin cabochons together with jump rings. With the front of one cabochon facing you, insert a jump ring through the right hole of a cabochon, and use flat-nose pliers to close the jump ring. (Consider using two pairs of pliers for this and the Connecting Jump Rings technique, page 72.)

25

21 With another resin cabochon, repeat step 20, but this time insert the jump ring through the hole on the left.

22 For the other two resin cabochons, secure jump rings to the holes on either side.

23 Connect all four cabochons together using additional jump rings in between them. The two resin cabochons on the ends should not have jump rings in the outside holes.

24 Thread beading wire through the hole on one outside cabochon, and secure with a crimp bead.

25 Start stringing beads onto the beading wire, making sure to cover the beading wire tail from the step above with beads, in the following order: one yellow bead, one red bead, one yellow bead, and one black bead.

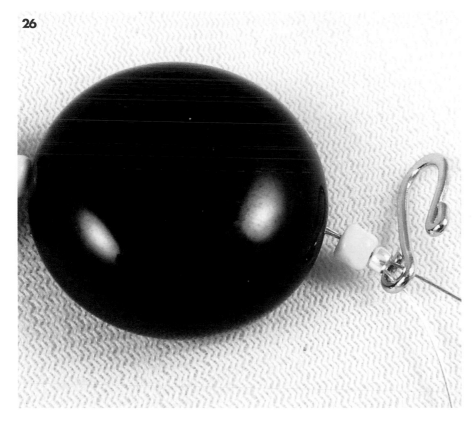

26

26 Continue to string beads in this pattern ending with one yellow bead, slip the end of the beading wire through one part of the hook-and-eye clasp, and secure it with another crimp bead.

27 Repeat steps 24 to 26 for the other side of the necklace.

Tip

When casting resin, consider making more than one piece of jewelry at a time since most molds have multiple compartments in them. This can be a time saver.

PRETTY COWGIRL FABRIC BELT BUCKLE

A colorful scrap of fabric is transformed into a resin and metal belt buckle in this surprisingly easy project. Reuse and recycle fabric swatches from old clothing or pick unusual textiles from a local fabric store's bargain bin. A little goes a long way in this belt buckle design that incorporates a few different resin techniques: Mixing, Pouring, and Top Coating.

1 Place a piece of paper over the top of the belt buckle, and with a pencil, trace around the inside of the buckle.

(continued)

YOU WILL NEED

- Envirotex Lite resin
- embossing gun
- scissors
- scrap paper and pencil
- fabric
- dry beans or rice
- belt buckle finding
- Aleene's Original Tacky Glue
- mixing cups and stir sticks
- waxed paper

1

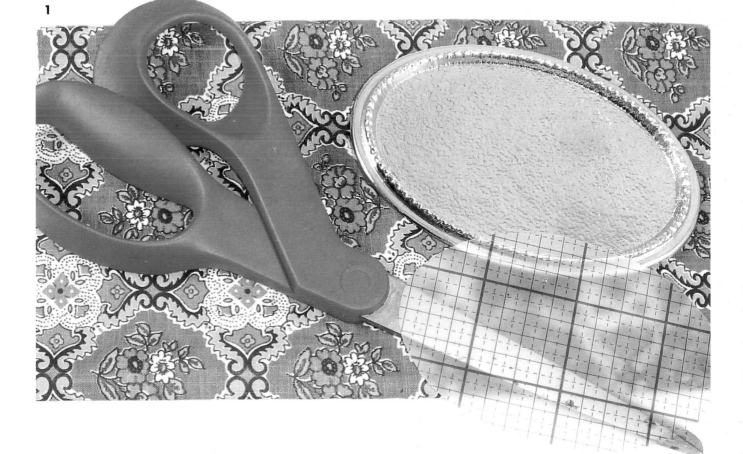

2 Cut out the template made in the previous step and then place it over your fabric piece. Cut around the template so that the fabric piece fits on top of the buckle.

3 Glue the fabric to buckle, and allow it to dry completely.

4 Place the buckle on top of a shallow pan of dry beans (or rice) to keep it even since the findings on the back of the buckle prevent it from laying flat.

5 Mix the Envirotex Lite resin (A), and pour it over the fabric, filling to the edge of the belt buckle (B).

6 If bubbles appear, lightly blow over them with an embossing gun or hair dryer. Be sure to go back and check your buckle 30 minutes to an hour later as air bubbles can form while the resin is hardening.

7 Allow the belt buckle to dry overnight in a place that is lint and debris free, such as an oven or under a box before attaching it to a belt.

MIXED MEDIA

The term "mixed media" in jewelry designing refers to the notion of combining an assortment of materials and techniques. Therefore, mixed-media doesn't really fit into one type of jewelry making or limit itself to a specific group of techniques. Just about any jewelry-making technique and material can be used together to create jewelry defined as mixed media, which is why this section is included at the end of this book. Any combination of ideas from previous sections, starting with bead stringing and ending with resin, will work for jewelry designers who are interested in creating mixed-media jewelry. Artist Cyndi Lavin has contributed technique ideas and projects to this section, providing additional crafting methods, such as stitching, stamping, and painting.

Tools and Supplies

While there are really no specific "must have" items to develop mixed-media jewelry, this section lists materials and tools necessary for making the projects included in this section as well as a few items that are just plain handy to have around. As with almost all forms of jewelry making, general tools such as pliers and wire cutters (also see the General Jewelry-Making Tools, page 9) are useful, but there are no hard and fast rules when it comes to mixed-media jewelry. Before acquiring additional tools and supplies, take a look at what you may already have around the house.

Sewing Tools: Sewing tools such as embroidery needles, beading needles, scissors, even a sewing machine, are helpful when stitching on extra adornments such as charms or beads or connecting fibers and other materials together.

Stamping Tools: Rubber stamps, an embossing gun and powders, and inks provide a fun way to alter the surface of items, such as polymer clay, resin, or wood beads.

Glues: Adhesives, glues, acrylic mediums, and two-part resins are all available at most craft stores and are excellent for sticking items together.

Painting Tools: Paintbrushes, sponge brushes, and acrylic paints are inexpensive and also offer a way to create unique backgrounds or other color details.

Paper: Collect little paper items such as fortunes from fortune cookies, business cards, tags, and other items normally discarded. An ephemera collection is inexpensive to create and provides inspiration as well as decorative possibilities. Pretty paper pieces, like those found in scrapbook stores, are also a good source for paper supplies.

Beading Threads and Needles: To stitch beads onto fabric or weave them together, a thin needle, called a beading needle, is necessary. This type of needle is longer and thinner than an average sewing needle. Beading threads such as Silamide and Nymo are also necessary. Silamide is twisted and comes prewaxed, but Nymo requires that it be pulled across a piece of wax to coat it.

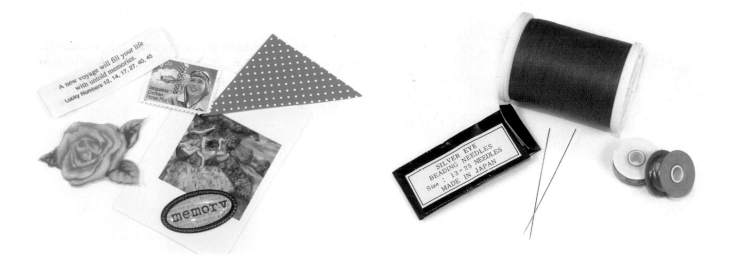

Beads: There is no "wrong" type of bead. Seed, resin, wood, ceramic, and gemstone beads all can be used to enhance mixed-media jewelry pieces.

Found Objects: Broken jewelry, shells, bottle caps, and more can be saved and repurposed for one-of-a-kind jewelry designs.

Fibers: Keep a little stash of yarn, ribbon, fabric strips, thread, cord, muslin, and fabric swatches to be incorporated into jewelry elements, such as rolled beads.

Jewelry Findings: As with just about any jewelry, findings are a must: clasps, jump rings, head pins, wire, pin backs, and earring wires are just some findings to have on hand.

Tip

A bottle of all-purpose tacky glue is just about indispensable for many mixed-media artists. Plus, it is readily available in most craft stores and is very inexpensive.

Techniques

As previously stated, don't limit yourself to these techniques. The crafting methods described in this section should be added to those already explained in this text or to others you may know already. There really is no limit to the type and number of methods used to make mixed-media jewelry.

BEADWORK

Edging Brick Stitch is a bead-weaving stitch that allows beads to be woven together without a loom or surface material, such as leather. It also works well to stitch around objects and cover raw edges, which is how it is demonstrated in this example. This form is called Edging Brick Stitch. The bead size can vary, but to make it easier to see how the stitch works, extra-large E-beads (about 4 mm) are used.

YOU WILL NEED

- beads
- beading needle
- beading thread
- fabric pieces

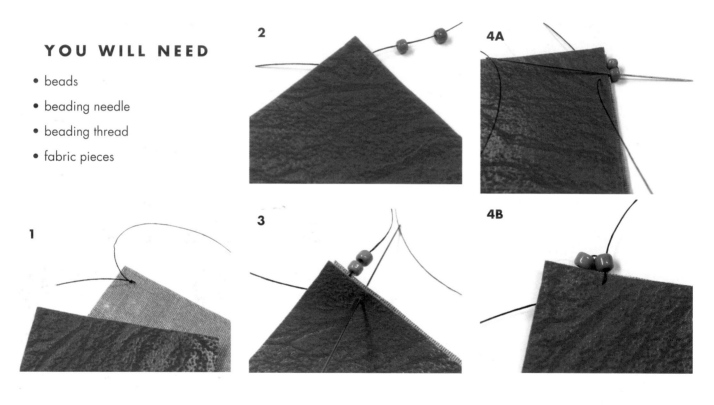

1 Knot the thread to the back of the fabric and pass the needle through to the front, up near the top edge. Place another piece of fabric on top of the first with wrong sides together.

2 Pick up two beads, and let them slide down to the fabric edges.

3 Stitch from back to front through both pieces of fabric directly underneath where the second bead will be. Make the stitches between ⅛" (3 mm) and ¼" (6 mm) in length, depending upon how much thread you want to show.

4 The holes of both beads will be perpendicular to the edge. Pass the needle up through the second bead (A) and pull the thread through (B).

5

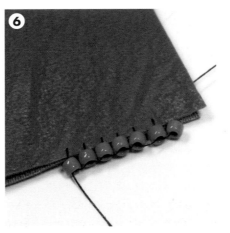

5 For each new stitch, string on only one bead up at a time, and pass the needle up through each new bead to get into position to add the next bead.

6 Eventually, the beads will create an edge around the fabric pieces. If stitching around the entire edge of the fabric pieces, make sure to pass the needle down through the first bead that was added and take a stitch back to front to set it in place.

Picot Stitch provides another way to create a cool embellishment to add on the edge of items. Before starting this stitch, first complete the Edging Brick Stitch.

1 Pass the needle up through one edging-brick-stitched bead.

2 Add an odd number of beads. Three is a good number, depending upon the size and the look desired, and stitch down through the next edging bead without catching the fabric.

3 Still without catching the fabric, pass the needle up through the next edging bead and repeat step 2.

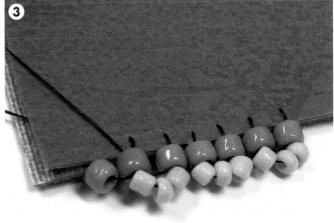

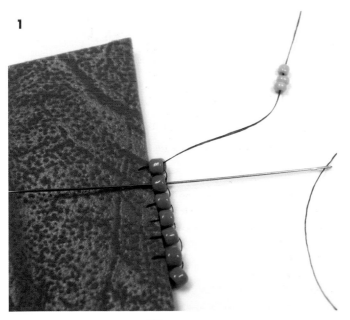

Bead Fringe adds dimension and texture to a mixed-media jewelry piece.

1 Knot the thread to the back of the fabric, pass the needle through to the front, and pick up as many beads as desired for the fringe.

2 Skip the top bead, and pass the needle down through the rest of the beads.

3 Pull the stack of beads against the fabric so that no loose thread is left at the top or the bottom, and pass the needle down through the fabric very close to where the thread came out.

4 Pull the tension on the thread to complete the first piece of fringe.

5 For extra stability, knot the thread to the back of the fabric after each stitch.

6 Repeat steps 1 to 5 to create multiple pieces of beaded fringe.

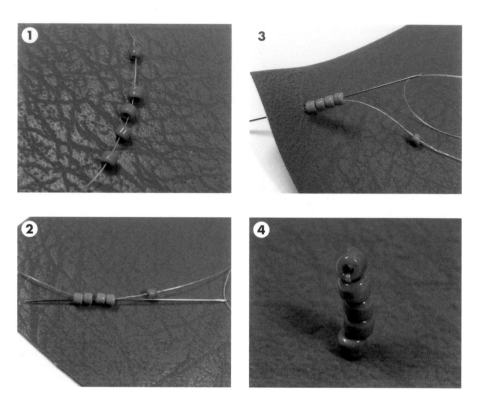

Loop Stitch is similar to fringe, but the idea is to create a loop or circle of beads that starts from one spot and loops around into that same spot on the surface being worked.

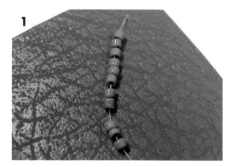
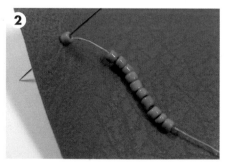

1 Knot the thread at the back of the fabric, pass the needle through to the front, and pick up an odd number of beads onto the beading needle.

2 Skip all the beads but the first, and pass the needle down through the first bead and the fabric very close to where the thread came out.

3 Pull the tension on the thread to complete the first beaded loop.

4 For extra stability, knot the thread to the back of the fabric after each stitch.

5 Repeat steps 1 to 4 to create multiple pieces of beaded loops.

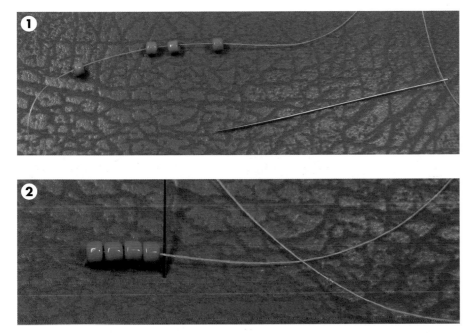

Back Stitch is a basic sewing stitch which, when combined with beads, can work as a way to frame components and add extra embellishments.

1 Knot the thread to the back of the fabric, pass the needle through to the front, and pick up two to five beads.

2 Bring the beads up snug against the thread, and insert the needle straight down through the fabric right after the last bead.

3 Pass the needle back up through the fabric in between two of the center beads in the group.

4 Insert the needle through the last half of the beads in the group, and pull the thread through snugly.

5 Pick up more beads and repeat from step 2, bringing the new group up snugly against the group just finished.

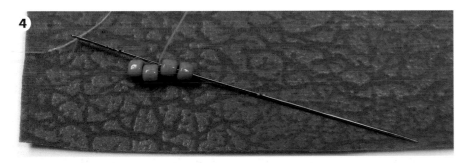

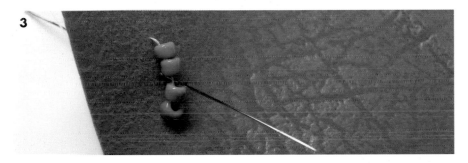

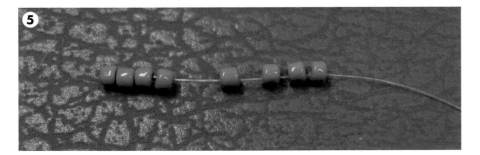

IMAGE TRANSFERS

Take a favorite picture or image and turn it into a piece of jewelry. It is possible with the use of this image transfer technique.

YOU WILL NEED

- muslin
- inkjet image printed out on inkjet transparency
- polymer medium in gloss finish
- foam brush
- bone folder or spoon
- small paintbrush
- walnut ink

3

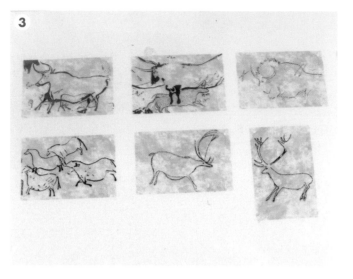

4

1

1 Cut out a piece of muslin, and if desired, fray the edges.

2 Print out an image on the rough side of a transparency.

3 Apply a thin layer of polymer medium (gloss) to the muslin, position the image on the muslin face down, and burnish it well with a bone folder or the back of spoon.

4 Remove the transparency, and if desired, coat the image with matte polymer medium to cut the shine.

5 Paint around the image with diluted walnut ink to blend the edges if needed.

Tip

Transparencies are available at most office supply stores as well as some craft stores.

ROLLED BEADS

Scraps of fabric or even paper can be easily transformed into beads. Then either string them "as is" or add them to other jewelry components. If desired, paint the paper or fabric, or choose fabric or paper that is already colored or has a pattern on it.

YOU WILL NEED

- fabric or paper
- scissors
- glue
- narrow drinking straws or stir tubes

1 Cut long thin rectangles of material the desired finished length of the bead.

2 Cut each rectangle in half diagonally into two triangles. Place them wrong side up.

3 Cut a straw into pieces slightly shorter than the narrow base of the triangles. Apply a dab of fabric glue to the narrow base of the triangle, and glue it to a straw. Roll the fabric around the straw, centering the fabric as you roll.

4 Add another dab of glue to seal the triangle tip to the bead.

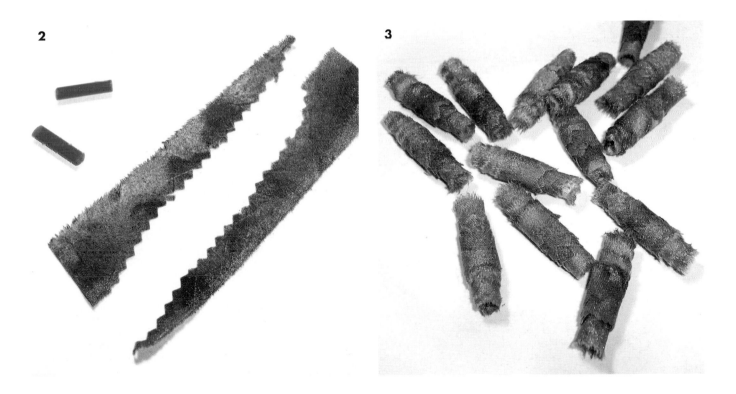

2

3

Tip

If making paper beads, roll long paper triangles around a wooden skewer or knitting needle but don't apply glue as you start. After gluing the tip to seal the bead, slide the bead off the skewer.

Projects

Mixed-media jewelry making is such a vast category, it might be difficult to decide where to start. These amazing projects, designed by Cyndi Lavin, are one place to begin. Follow the directions exactly or use them as inspiration to create totally different looks for your jewelry pieces.

MEASURE ME BRACELET

An antique tape measure is the inspiration behind this cuff bracelet that mixes fiber with bead-weaving techniques and a little glue. The result is this exquisite bracelet.

YOU WILL NEED

- cuff bracelet blank
- antique cloth tape measure
- thin cotton batting
- 10 g of size 8/0 seed beads
- 10 g of size 11/0 seed beads
- beading thread, such as Silamide
- fabric glue
- alligator clips
- size 12 beading needle

1

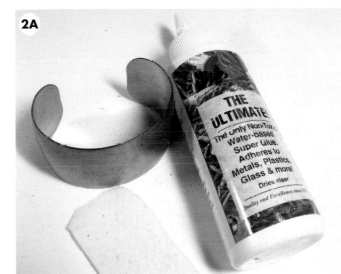

2A

2B

1 Cut a piece of thin batting to fit the outside of the bracelet blank.

2 Glue the batting in place with a few drops of fabric glue.

3 Wrap the tape measure around the blank, making sure each wrap overlaps the previous one slightly.

4 Add a small dab of fabric glue to the end of the tape, turn the end of the tape under, and use alligator clips to hold it in place until it is dry.

5 Use size 8/0 seed beads and the Edging Brick Stitch technique (page 260), bead along the entire edge of the cuff.

6 Use the smaller 11/0 beads, three beads for each stitch, and the Picot Stitch technique (page 261) to add a final row of beads around the cuff.

SUMMER DREAM NECKLACE

Why just dream about beautiful jewelry when you can have fun crafting it? Rubber stamping lovers will especially enjoy this project, which incorporates simple stamping and painting methods with a few fiber techniques.

1A

1B

YOU WILL NEED

- piece of wire
- sea sponge
- heat gun
- alphabet stamp
- scissors
- tweezers
- five 25-mm flat rectangle resin beads
- ten 10-mm drum resin beads
- fifteen 10-mm round resin beads
- Lumiere by Jacquard acrylic paints in citrine and halo pink gold
- solvent ink
- StazOn ink pad in jet black
- pink C-Lon cord
- liquid seam sealant
- eight size 8/0 or 6/0 triangular pink resin beads
- clear-drying cement

1 Suspend all the resin beads on wire to paint (A), and dab the beads with acrylics using a sea sponge, making sure to allow a little of the original color of the beads to peek through (B).

(continued)

2

2 When the beads are dry, stamp the surface of the five flat beads to spell out "DREAM." When they are dry, flip the beads over and stamp the other side too.

3 Cut two 36" (91 cm) pieces of C-Lon cord, and coat the tips of each piece with seam sealant.

4 Hold both cords together so that you are using a double strand, string on the middle flat bead created in step 2 (the "E" bead), push it to the middle of the cords, and tie an overhand knot (page 206) on each side of the bead. Make sure to slide the bead up tightly against the knot. Use a pair of tweezers or an awl if necessary.

5 After the "E" bead is in the center, string on a drum bead, and make another knot after it.

6 Continue to add beads and knot between each one in the following order moving out from the center of the necklace: flat "A" bead; one drum bead; flat "M" bead; three drum beads; and seven round beads.

7 Starting back at the "E" bead and moving in the opposite direction from the string completed in step 6, continue to add beads and knot between each one in this order moving out from the center of the necklace: one drum bead; flat "R" bead; one drum bead; flat "D" bead; three drum beads; and seven round beads.

8 Cut two 24" (60.9 cm) pieces of C-Lon cord.

9

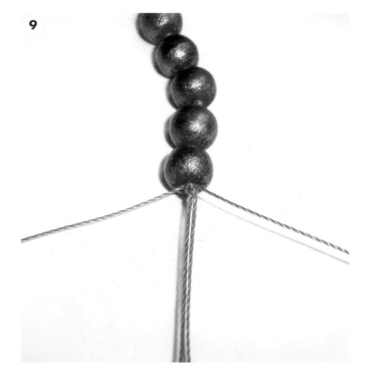

9 Place one of the new cord pieces from step 8 between the original two cords from steps 3 and 4 emerging from one of the necklace ends. Using the previous two strands from steps 3 and 4, tie another knot around the new cord, using the original two cords and sliding the knot up tightly against the last bead to trap the new cord in place.

12

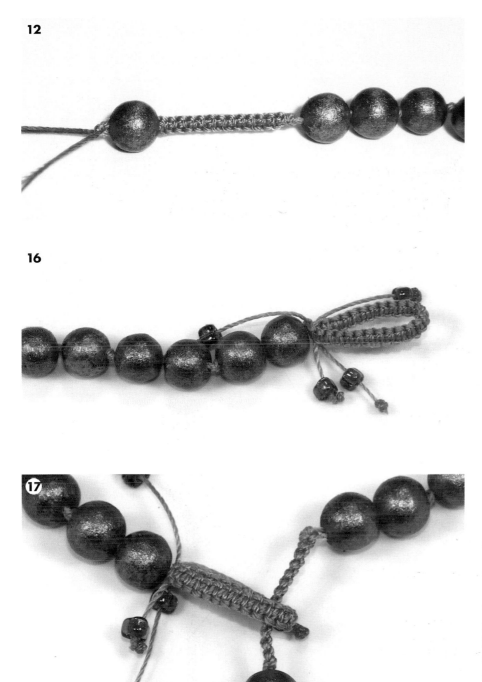

16

17

10 Slide the cord until it is trapped at the halfway point.

11 Using the longer cords, tie square macramé knots (page 207) around the middle two strands for about 1" (2.5 cm).

12 Take all four strands through the last 10-mm bead and knot into place using another square knot.

13 Repeat steps 9 and 10 on the other end of the necklace.

14 Repeat step 11, but make this knotted section long enough to create a loop that the 10-mm bead will fit through.

15 Use a square knot to tie the loose ends securely around the base of the knotted section.

16 Thread a triangle bead on each cord end and knot it in place using an overhand knot.

17 Apply cement to each knot and allow them to dry before clipping off the excess cord.

Tip

When stamping on a surface with a rubber stamp, avoid rocking the stamp back and forth. It is better to press firmly and then pull up. Otherwise, the rocking motion can create shadows or double marks from the stamp.

ALWAYS TIME FOR CATS BRACELET

Steampunk jewelry incorporates mechanical found objects, such as watch parts and small gears, into one-of-a-kind pieces that have an old-world, edgy attitude. Here's a bracelet that fits right in with this popular jewelry style. If cats aren't your favorite subject, use other images for your bracelet.

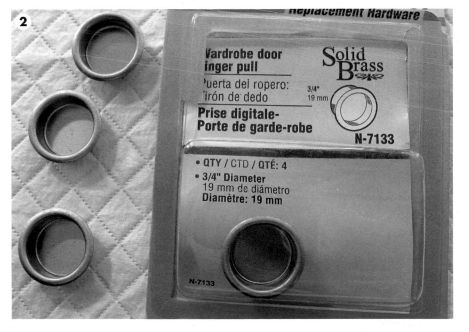

YOU WILL NEED

- disk-and-loop bracelet, brass
- watch face parts
- seed bead assortment
- epoxy 330
- black beading thread, such as Silamide or Nymo
- beading needles, size 12
- scraps of Ultrasuede
- flat-back rhinestones
- three ¾" (1.9 cm) sliding closet door pulls
- three ¾" (1.9 cm) cat images
- scissors

1 Prepare the cat images by cutting them out so that they are ¾" (1.9 cm) circles.

2 Mix the epoxy and fill the closet pulls half way.

3 Let it set for a few minutes and carefully place the images in the pulls.

4 Fill the pulls to the top and let them dry and harden overnight. (Epoxy dries quickly, but it's still good to let it cure for a while.)

(continued)

5 Glue the epoxy images to small scraps of Ultrasuede.

6 While the epoxy pieces dry, work on creating four groups of clock parts by using a round watch face for the bottom, and layering the other watch parts and a few flat-backed rhinestones on top. Use glue to attach all the pieces together, and allow them to dry thoroughly.

7 Once the glue has dried, use the Back Stitch technique (page 263) and size 11/0 seed beads to stitch two rows around the edges of the pulls.

8 Next use the Loop Stitch (page 262) and Forming Fringe (page 262) techniques to stitch an assortment of loops and fringe, anchoring them to the first row of back stitch created in step 7. Use about eleven seed beads for each loop and six seed beads for each fringe piece, and alternate between these two stitches while working around the slide. This will create a lot of texture, suggesting cat whiskers and fur.

9 Clip the Ultrasuede close to the outer circle of beads, and use the Picot Stitch technique (page 261) to stitch a small three-bead picot over every other bead around the second row of back stitch created in step 7.

10 Glue another piece of Ultrasuede to the bottom of each embroidered piece to hide the stitches.

11 When the glue is dry, carefully clip the bottom piece of fabric even with the top piece.

12 Determine the orientation of each piece before attaching it to the bracelet (A), and then glue the watch parts and beaded images to the bracelet disks (B).

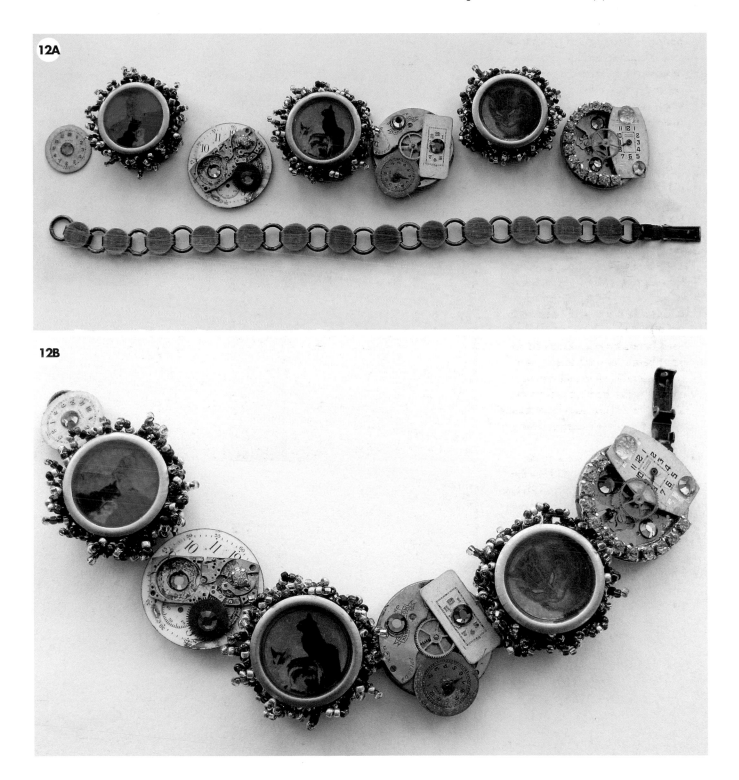

12A

12B

RUSTIC TRANSFER NECKLACE

This necklace is new, but it looks like an artifact excavated from ancient ruins. And it is all due to the materials and techniques of mixed media, including making rolled beads from fabric and transferring images. Some bead-weaving stitches also provide some added embellishments.

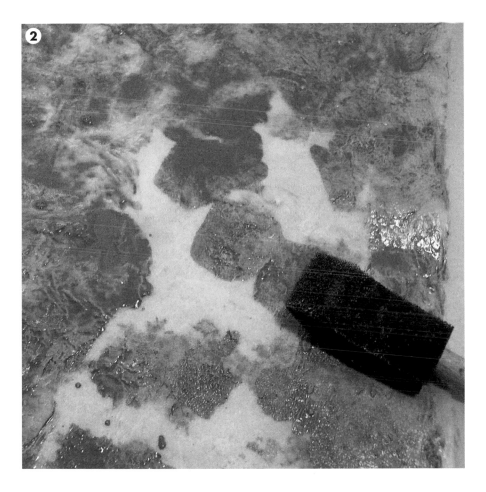

1 Create faux leather by ironing fusible web to the felt, and then smear the surface with acrylic gels. Allow it to partially dry before continuing.

2 Drip a light paint color onto the felt and dab it lightly with a foam brush.

3 Repeat step 2 using other paint colors, layering until the piece is covered.

(continued)

YOU WILL NEED

- square of white felt
- fusible web
- extra heavy acrylic gel
- soft acrylic gel
- acrylic paints: raw sienna, burnt sienna, interference gold
- iron
- parchment paper
- foam brush
- paper towel
- heat gun
- muslin
- inkjet image printed out on inkjet transparency
- polymer medium
- bone folder or spoon
- walnut ink
- scissors
- glue
- drinking straws
- Ultrasuede
- fabric glue
- beads of various sizes, including 11/0 seed beads
- yarn in shades of brown and rust
- beading needle
- 24" to 30" (60 to 76 cm) 2-mm black leather cord
- two 10-mm bamboo beads
- one 18 × 6.5-mm copper tube-top bail
- tacky glue

4 When the felt is almost dry, spread on a light layer of interference gold, and dab lightly with a paper towel. Let it dry thoroughly before using.

5 Use the Image Transfer technique, page 264, to transfer your choice of antique image, such as a buffalo, to a piece of muslin, fray the edges of the muslin, and coat the image with matte polymer medium.

6 While this is drying, use the same acrylic paints used for the faux leather to paint some muslin.

7 After the fabric from step 6 has dried, use it to form three beads using the Rolled Beads technique, page 265.

8

8 To assemble the necklace, cut out a piece of the faux leather made in steps 1 to 4 so that it is about 1" (2.5 cm) larger in diameter than the image transfer.

9 Holding the image transfer against a piece of faux leather, take a needle and thread, tie a knot on the end of the thread, and bring the needle through the back of both pieces.

10 Add one bead of any size other than a seed bead, and then add a seed bead.

11 Skip the seed bead, and bring the needle down through the first bead and back through both pieces of fabric.

12 Repeat steps 9 to 11 to anchor all four corners of the transfer, and add more beads to background if desired.

13 Double a strand of yarn, and make an overhand knot to form a loop on one end of the yarn piece.

14 String a fabric bead onto the doubled yarn, and make another overhand knot just past the fabric bead.

15 Repeat steps 13 and 14 for the other two fabric beads.

16 Stitch the looped yarn of all three fabric bead pieces to the back of the faux leather.

16

17 Cut a backing piece of Ultrasuede the same size as the faux leather piece previously made, hold both pieces together, and use 11/0 seed beads to add an Edging Brick Stitch, page 260, all around the outside edges

18 Next, decorate it with a row of Picot Stitch, page 261, using 11/0 seed beads, three beads for each stitch.

19 Use tacky glue to adhere the copper bail to the back of the Ultrasuede. Allow the glue to dry.

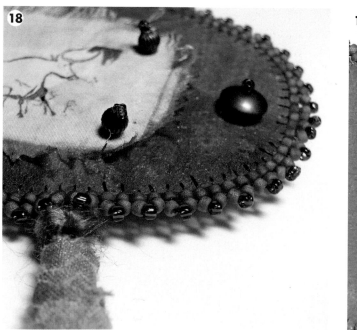

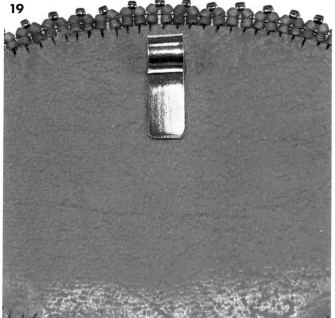

20

21

22

20 Fold the leather cord in half, and make an overhund knot about ¾" (1.9 cm) from the folded leather end.

21 Slide the loose ends of the doubled cord through the copper bail.

22 Add two bamboo beads to the loose ends of the cord, adding overhand knots on either side of each bead to secure them. This will create a toggle-style clasp.

Jewelry Gallery

Become inspired in this gallery of amazing jewelry designs created by an assortment of jewelry artists who have used a plethora of techniques from bead stringing to metal work and more. After viewing these gallery pages, move onto these designers' web sites, and start imagining the jewelry pieces that will encompass your own distinctive perspective.

Kenneth Fron
www.kennethfron.com
"Orange Sea Glass"
Irregularly shaped frosted orange sea glass beads make this 25 inch one-of-a-kind necklace pop! Gold-tone beads alternate between the sea glass beads and are finished off with crimp beads and a barrel clasp.

Cyndi Lavin, Mazel Tov! Jewelry Treasures
www.mazeltovjewelry.com
"Silver Sparkle Pendant"
This polymer clay cabochon was formed using a combination of silver leaf, black polymer clay, and acrylic paint. The back is finished off with ultra suede and a bail made of seed beads while the bezel around the sides was created using a colorful mix of glass seed beads.

Kathy Pine, Owner & Designer, WorldWise Jewelry
www.worldwisejewelry.com

"Lace and Pearls"

Soft colors of pink, gray, peach, and white pearls are woven into hairpin lace around a handcrafted fine silver bracelet frame. This cuff bracelet makes a beautifully feminine statement.

Artisan Fine Silver Jewelry by Melissa J. Lee
www.melissajlee.com

"Cubism"

The design for this dramatic necklace started with the floating box pendant made from metal clay and adorned with pieces of sea glass in the center. The toggle clasp is also from metal clay. The double strand of beads include amber, faceted garnet, faceted amethyst, green amber, Chinese turquoise, and hessonite garnet, which dangles from the floating box pendant.

"Gothic Pink"

Grunge never looked so pretty in a bracelet. This design includes a mixture of pink Lucite rose beads, black rondelle beads, faceted black glass beads, and a metal clay skull charm and button toggle clasp.

(continued)

Melissa J. Lee (continued)
"I Think Therefore I Am 1.0"
A thick leather cord secures chain and long metal clay charms around the perimeter of the necklace. Binary code – "I Think Therefore I Am" – is stamped on each metal clay piece. The faceted green stones are dark peridot.

"Stop Traffic"
Chunky faceted black onyx beads encircle this bracelet that is accented with metal clay and resin charms in the color of a traffic light: green, yellow, and red. The textured toggle clasp was also made using metal clay.

"HRH Princess Charming"
This triple strand necklace includes a huge array of materials: white, peach, and pink pearls, peridot, Madagascar rose quartz, pink opal, quartz crystals, round and faceted rose quartz, white seed beads, and rose satin Swarovski crystals. The artist made the clasp and letter charms using metal clay and used a focal lampwork bead made by Lezlie Belanger and attached it to a metal clay base.

Mixed Media Jewelry by Liz Revit
www.lizrevit.blogspot.com
"Yours Truly"
Strands of ribbon, accented with glass beads, are woven through links on antiqued chain in this mixed media jewelry piece. The pendants were formed by first tea-staining muslin and then stitching small piece of the muslin together using needle, thread, and seed beads.

(continued)

Liz Revit (continued)
"Awakening"

A glazed pottery butterfly pendant is enhanced with a mix of beads including Miyuki seed beads and Delicas, Swarovski crystal bicones, and assorted sizes of silver-colored spacer beads. The brown silk cord is knotted here and there throughout the necklace.

Judy Kogut
"Kazuri Necklace"

Wire, beading, and metal clay techniques are combined in this stunning necklace. The wire straps are woven with acrylic silver-colored wire, and the center beads include Kazuri Beads, sterling silver beads, and crystal beads. The flower pendant is made of metal clay.

Sterling Silver Jewelry by Victoria Tillotson
www.victoriatillotson.com
"Turquoise Statement"

This turquoise cabochon ring is part of the artist's "Statement" collection. The large cabochon is set in an oval bezel and the ring band was textured using a ball peen hammer.

"Square Upon Square"
Textured squares frame highly polished squares in these dramatic sterling silver earrings.

"Citrine Statement"
Also part of the "Statement" collection, this faceted citrine ring is set in a large bezel and band that have been pierced with tiny holes throughout.

"Double Dangle Teardrops"
Large textured sterling teardrops frame smaller teardrop dangles in these powerful earrings.

(continued)

Victoria Tillotson (continued)
"Hinge on It"
Sterling silver and 18kt gold make up this hinged cuff bracelet that includes a box-style clasp.

"Tourmalated Time"
A square cut tourmalated quartz cabochon is housed in a sterling bezel with hinge-style ring band accented with 18kt gold.

"Ring Assortment"
This sterling silver ring assortment includes a variety of small bezel set cabochons: Rutilated quartz, lapis, carnelian, amethyst, peridot, and black onyx.

Melanie Brooks, Earthenwood Studio
www.earthenwoodstudio.com
"Woodland Mermaid Necklace"
Double strands of intricate chain are connected to an assortment of beads and dangles in this fantasy-themed necklace: hand-crafted porcelain beads, wooden components, metal beads, and crystals.

Jean Yates
http://prettykittydogmoonjewelry.
blogspot.com/
"Snow Princess"

Five silver coated leaves and enamel snow flake charms are centered on this double strand necklace. Beads and other ornaments spaced around the necklace include dichroic beads, CZ charms, tiny Hill Tribe beads, and Swarovski crystals. The toggle clasp is finished with an enamel charm as well.

Jewelry Art by Andrew Thornton
http://andrew-thornton.blogspot.com/
"Persephone's Folly"

This unusual chain is fine silver. The flower shaped links and round links were made using metal clay; then finished off with some wire wrapped cubic zirconia beads and a pretty pewter flower and leaf clasp.

"Hawaiian Memories"
Souvenir pennies collected by the artist while on a trip to Hawaii were the inspiration for this bracelet that is so full of movement it actually tinkles when worn. Along with the pennies that came from penny press machines, other materials include pewter shell beads and a pewter Shibuichi clasp, Peruvian opal, pearls, coral, brass, glass, crystals, and copper.

"The Hierophant's Daughter"
This bracelet is a mixture of basic chain maille techniques, copper clay, and filigree. The silver jump rings have been oxidized for an earthy look that goes with the copper and pewter clasp.

(continued)

Andrew Thornton (continued)
"From Fathoms Deep"
Eye popping materials make this deceptively simple beaded bracelet look amazing. Many of the materials were made by fellow jewelry artists: polymer clay beads by Pam and Heather Wynn; pewter beads and clasp from Green Girl Studios; ceramic beads by Keith O'Connor; and drilled beach glass from Stephanie Ann.

Vintage and Mixed-Media Jewelry by Chari Auerbach
"Vintage Cap Chandelier Earrings"
Vintage bead caps are used to dangle loads of crystal beads and create these chandelier earrings. Two tones of turquoise beads are also mixed together in these long earrings.

"Venice Meets Vintage"
Venetian glass beads and crystal beads are combined in a colorful pattern of purple, blue, and black and accented with vintage bead caps. It is finished off with a magnetic clasp.

"More than Memories"
Crystal beads and marquee shaped crystals once adorned a jacket found by the artist in a thrift store. Now they are strung on two strands of memory wire for a bright red bangle design.

(continued)

Chari Auerbach (continued)
"All Kinds of Pink"

A menagerie of pink makes up this collection of beads that is connected with wrapped titanium wire. Beads include crystals, rhodonite, furnace glass, and pressed glass.

"Recycled Mixed Media"

From antique coral found on a broken estate sale necklace to odds and ends of metal components and chunky amber beads that came from who knows where, this super long necklace is dramatic and very eclectic. Glass and agate stone beads are also sprinkled throughout the mix.

Fiber and Bead Jewelry by Terry L. Carter
http://tappingflamingo.blogspot.com/
"Floral Fun Fiber"
Small glass seed beads are interspersed between crochet stitches on natural cotton thread to create the straps of this necklace. The center component is a blown glass floral-motif borealis pendant.

"Connect the Dots"
Round ceramic beads in shades of blue, pink, and gray are connected with cotton thread using a basic crochet technique. The beads are spaced out between single crochet and finished off with a spring ring clasp.

Chain and Coin Jewelry by Michael V. Powley
"Eagle Eye"
A massive amount of sterling silver jump rings make up this long Byzantine patterned chain maille necklace. The pendant includes a coin bezel around an 1847 ten dollar eagle coin.

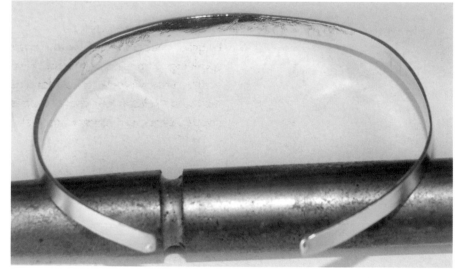

"Anniversary Cuff Bracelet"
Originally a gold American Eagle coin, this 22kt cuff bracelet was fabricated by using a hammer to pound it repeatedly to form the gold into a semi-circle. This was a 20 year anniversary gift and includes an inscription inside of the cuff with the original wedding dates and initials of the artist and his wife.

"We Are United"
This ring was once a silver Benjamin Franklin half dollar and was transformed into a band-style ring by repeated hammerings and forming around a ring mandrel. It still includes raised lettering inside that says "United States of America."

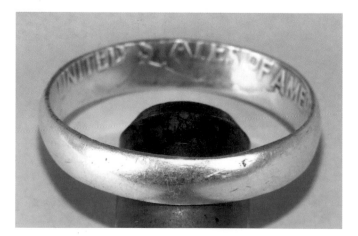

Wire and Bead Jewelry
by Tammy Powley
"Rockin' Ruby Zoisite"
Chunky ruby zoisite 15mm by 32mm beads are wire wrapped with copper. The coil elements secure the bottom of the beads as well as decorate the top, which is connected to hand-fabricated copper ear hooks.

"Royal Vintage Bracelet"
Filigree bead caps hold each sparkling purple crystal bead. Plus, a tiny brass vintage locket dangles next to a skeleton key charm on this copper, brass, and crystal bracelet.

Jewelry Supply Resources

Rio Grande
Web site: www.riogrande.com

Equipment, beads, metal,
and other related jewelry supplies

Artbeads
Web site: www.artbeads.com

Artgems, Inc
Web site: www.artgems.com

Auntie's Beads
Web site: www.auntiesbeads.com

Beadshop
Web site: www.beadshop.com

The Bead Warehouse
Web site:
www.thebeadwarehouse.com

B'Sue Boutique
Web site: www.bsueboutiques.com

CGM
Web site: www.cgmfindings.com

D.D. Hess Glass Beads
Web site: www.ddhess.com

Dick Blick Art Supplies
Web site: www.dickblick.com

General crafts supplies
Web site: www.gemshow-online.com

Fire Mountain Gems and Beads
Web site: www.firemountaingems.com

HHH Enterprises
Web site: www.hhhenterprises.com

Jan's Jewels
Web site: www.jansjewels.com

JSBeads.com
Web site: www.jsbeads.com

Land of Odds
Web site: www.landofodds.com

Monsterslayer
Web site: www.monsterslayer.com

Ornamentea
Web site: www.ornamentea.com

Out on a Whim
Web site: www.whimbeads.com

Rings and Things
Web site: www.rings-things.com

Shipwreck Beads
Web site: www.shipwreckbeads.com

Soft Flex Company
Web site: www.softflextm.com

South Pacific Wholesale Co.
Web site: www.beading.com

Tripp's
Web site: www.tripps.com

Urban Maille Chainworks
Web site: www.urbanmaille.com

WigJig
Web site: www.wigjig.com

International Sources
for Jewelry-Making Supplies

African Trade Beads
Web site:
www.africantradebeads.com

Beads Unlimited
Web site: www.beadsunlimited.co.uk

Beadfx
Web site: www.beadfx.com

Beadgems
Web site: www.beadgems.com

The Bead Shop
Web site: www.beadshop.co.uk

Canadian Beading Supply
Web site: www.canbead.com

Gems2Behold
Web site: www.gems2behold.com

The House of Orange
Web site: www.houseoforange.biz

Katie's Treasures
Web site: www.katiestreasures.com.au

Kernowcrafts Rocks
and Gems Limited
Web site: www.kernowcraft.com

Gem Craft
Web site: www.gemcraft.co.uk

Space Trader
Web site: www.spacetrader.com.au

Participating Jewelry Designers

POLYMER CLAY AND MIXED-MEDIA SECTIONS

Cyndi Lavin is a mixed media artist, jewelry designer, and writer living in central Massachusetts. She strongly believes that life and art are intertwined, that we are all works of art, designed to be creative beings, and that life consists of discovering the things that we are meant to create. Cyndi's work appears in many art and jewelry books as well as in popular magazines like *Belle Armoire, Simply Beads, Life Images,* and *Somerset Digital Images.* She enjoys sharing her art adventures and tutorials through her daily blogs: www.beading-arts.com and www.mixed-media-artist.com.

RESIN SECTION

Jennifer Perkins is the woman behind the jewelry label, book, and blog: Naughty Secretary Club (www.naughtysecretaryclub.com). She is a founding member of the Austin Craft Mafia, the host of *Craft Lab,* and a compulsive thrift store shopper. Jennifer lives, teaches, and crafts in Austin, Texas, with her husband and daughter, whom she plans to teach to craft just as soon as she can hold a pair of safety scissors.

CHAIN MAKING, FABRICATION, AND SOLDERING SECTIONS

Michael V. Powley, the author's husband, collaborated on many of the designs and information provided in this text, especially when it came to working with metal. In addition to creating many of the jewelry pieces, he is also responsible for photographing the majority of the step-by-step images throughout. His day job as a civil engineer has given him an eye for detail that is especially important when it comes to metal work.

Acknowledgments

Thank you to the team at Creative Publishing international for its help on this project. Linda Neubauer, my editor, has been wonderful about answering all my questions and guiding me through this process. I want to also thank Winnie Prentiss for remembering me when it came to the author search for this book.

Michael V. Powley, my husband and best friend, has given up countless weekends and holidays to take photographs, design projects, and provide technical editing help. I'm sure he is glad to get his life back!

Cyndi Lavin and Jennifer Perkins took a huge load off of my shoulders when they agreed to help with some of the sections in this book. Their talent and expertise added a great deal to the final product.

The jewelry designers who sent in their special jewelry pieces for the gallery gave this book that final "touch" it needed. Their generosity is very much appreciated.

Rio Grande also deserves a big thank you for allowing me to use a large number of high-resolution color images of jewelry-making supplies and equipment from the company's catalogs and web site.

About the Author

Tammy Powley is a writer, designer, and teacher. She has been a long-time crafter working in all kinds of media from fiber arts to glass. After spending eight years on the art show circuit selling her jewelry designs as well as supplying small boutiques with her work, she began writing about her crafting experiences and focusing on teaching others how to make jewelry. She is the author of numerous jewelry-making books, and has an extensive background in writing for the web—she has been About.com's Guide to Jewelry Making expert since 1989. Tammy has a Ph.D. in Texts and Technology, and as her "day job," she teaches college English, primarily composition, literature, and technical communications. See her web site at http://www.tammypowley. com for more information.

Index